TRAD...
B...
A...
CI...
MAKING

By the same author

Wine Making The Natural Way
Wine Making With Herbs

TRADITIONAL BEER AND CIDER MAKING

Ian Ball

RIGHT WAY

Contents

Chapter	Page

INTRODUCTION

WHY BREW?

Pub beer is worse than ever. Never in English history has so much money been charged for such weak, gassy brews.

Never has our choice of ale and beer been so limited. Even the "real" ales, boasted by breweries today, would have been tipped down the drain by our great grandfathers.

We are told our quality of life has never been so good. Maybe, but one thing is certain, our ale and beer have never been so bad.

Traditional and modern ales and beers brewed to the recipes and simple instructions given in this book leave pub beer way behind in quality and you have a wide selection of types of ale, beer, lager and stout to choose from. All the brews can be made from pure, natural ingredients, without adding chemicals or sugar (sucrose) and your beer can be bottled or barrelled and ready for enjoyable drinking within a few weeks of making it. In addition you can adjust flavours, textures and strengths to suit every occasion, as did our ancestors.

Many of the ancient brews revived here were once an essential part of English daily life and diet, but time-honoured methods of making beer which they embodied were forced out of existence by the large breweries' mediocre, mass-produced beer. Nowadays such recipes are unlikely to be found elsewhere.

Brew your favourite modern beer; sample the ale King Alfred enjoyed, the sack Shakespeare's characters loved, the herb ale Queen Elizabeth I drank and many other traditional country ales and beers brewed for centuries to bestow good health (and long life!) on the drinker.

Making your own beer is easy, takes little time and the finest pint costs only a fraction of the price you would expect to pay over a bar.

Having home-brewed ales, stouts, ciders or whatever available means you may quench your thirst whenever you like; hold inexpensive home brew parties; take your social life *home*, away from pubs, smokey bars, noisy computer games and rowdy aggressors.

Enjoy beer with your meals and use it for preparing and flavouring exciting new dishes. Some superb recipes are included in Chapter 14, starting on page 48.

Home brewed beers are full of vitamins, nourishment and energy-giving goodness. A pint of country style, traditional brew has a higher energy value than a pint of milk and accompanied by a

hunk of fresh, crusty wholemeal bread and a slice of cheese is a satisfying, nutritionally excellent meal.

To enable you to locate brewing methods instantly an easy-to-use index is given on page 57.

Cider, made from fermented apple juice, has ancient and sacred associations with pre-Christian religious ceremonies. Cider was regarded as a sacred beverage that possessed special health-promoting and healing qualities, and was believed to bring happiness and love into the lives of those people who drank it.

Cider was the traditional drink of the Celts in Britain, and as the Anglo-Saxon settlers from Germany gradually occupied England and forced the Celts into Wales and the west country in the fifth century A.D., the displaced Celts took with them their cider making secrets and techniques and continued to plant and care for their orchards and sacred groves of cider apple trees.

The craft of cider making was also continued in Gloucestershire, Herefordshire, Kent and Norfolk. An old Herefordshire legend states that if a cider apple orchard is destroyed to make way for a field of hops to flavour ale or beer, it will be cursed and the venture doomed to failure.

Cider production in Britain reached a peak in the seventeenth century, when large shipments of cider were taken to London, where good quality cider was preferred to medium grade French wine.

Cider was, however, never as popular as ale or beer and heavy taxes levied on cider steadily reduced public demand to the point where, by the eighteenth century, commercial apple growing and cider production was in rapid decline. Today, however, cider is enjoying a revival in popularity and commercial cider made in Devon and Somerset is renowned world-wide for its high quality.

Few rustic crafts can be more ideally suited for those of us who enjoy making things ourselves, or be blessed with more tangible results!

Cider made at home is an economical and delicious beverage with all the natural goodness of apples.

In this book cider making begins at Chapter 20 and *there is a special quick index to help you locate principles and methods on page 108.*

1

BEFORE BEER

In the beginning was ale. Beer came a hop later.

Ale is the traditional English drink. Anglo-Saxon settlers brought it with them from their German homelands in the fifth century A.D.

Ale was brewed from barley and flavoured with honey, flowers, fruit and herbs. There were many kinds of ale and it was drunk for pleasure, nourishment, health and fitness.

Ale was enjoyed in large quantities at social gatherings. It formed an important part of daily diet and nutritional intake, and addition of medicinal herbs gave ale a highly valued healing quality.

The Romans, who frequently warred with Angles and Saxons, noted how they often drank ale before battle and fought like demons.

Vikings also drank a honeyed ale before going berserk in battle. Berserkers were Vikings who led attacks. Their courage and indifference to wounds and pain is legendary.

Ale played an important part in every aspect of English daily life.

Beer came to England a thousand years later. It was introduced by Dutch protestant refugees, who drank a weak ale, flavoured with bitter tasting hops, which preserved it in storage. They called this drink beer.

Initially, beer was universally disliked by Englishmen, who regarded it as an insipid, sleep inducing, fattening brew. And "beer guts" was a term of abuse applied to the fat Dutchmen.

Beer was not as strong or nourishing as honey, herb, flower and fruit flavoured ales.

Today, the only distinction between *commercial* beer and ale is the lighter colour and hopping of some ales compared with bitter beer. Often, there is no discernible difference.

With this book, as well as brewing modern ales, beers, stout and lager, you have the opportunity to sample some of the lost olde ales of Merrie England.

Of course you are not allowed to *sell* your home-made beers and ciders; for this you would need a special licence by arrangement (in the U.K.) with H.M. Customs and Excise. Home-made brews are therefore only for consumption by yourself and your family and guests to whom you serve them.

2

BRIEF HISTORY

Ale was brewed in ancient Mesopotamia in 800 B.C. Laws were passed governing its sale by tavern keepers.

It was also taxed!

The ancient Egyptians believed Osiris, god of agriculture, taught humans the secret of successful brewing. They recorded several recipes.

Ale was known to the ancient Greeks and Romans. The Romans occasionally drank hopped ale, or beer. However, inhabitants of vine growing countries preferred wine to ale.

When wine sipping Normans invaded England in 1066, they

found ale quaffing Saxons with well established breweries and ale houses.

The Domesday Book, compiled in 1086, records the existence of forty-three sizeable breweries in England. Saxon recipes suggest their ale was at least three times stronger than modern beer.

Most households brewed ale. Brewing was a woman's work and the wife was brewmistress.

Norman aristocrats continued drinking French wines; Saxons preferred ale.

Drinking competitions were held regularly and a Saxon's manliness was judged by the amount of ale he could drink. Pegs fitted into tankards marked the amount of ale to be drunk in one swallow. The longer a contest lasted the higher pegs were raised. This is the origin of the phrase, "to bring him down a peg or two." If an opponent could no longer compete, his pegs were lowered. But this type of contest is certainly not to be recommended today; we know more about the health risks!

Pubs began as ordinary houses alongside much-travelled routes where the good wife, to earn a few pence towards housekeeping, brewed ale and offered it for sale to thirsty, travel-worn passers-by. A broom was stood outside the house as a sign that ale was sold. Brooms were probably the first pub signs.

Ale was first taxed nationally in the twelfth century. Quality and prices were firmly controlled in the thirteenth century, when official ale tasters were appointed to sample and approve a brew before it could be sold. There was considerable competition for their jobs!

Oxford and Cambridge University Colleges were busy brewing their own distinctive ales in the fourteenth century and the Church joined in on a large scale in the fifteenth century. Justices of the peace were given power to grant and revoke licences to ale houses and innkeepers. Hopped beer made an appearance.

In the sixteenth century Dutch settlers planted hop fields in Kent. The Church reduced ale production and breweries increased supplies to ale houses, inns and taverns – many had previously brewed their own ale. Exports of ale were made to France, where it was favourably compared with medium quality wine.

Tax on ale and beer was considerably increased in the seventeenth century and became a major source of Government revenue. Many families still brewed their own supply of ale and beer for mealtimes.

The eighteenth century saw the formation of large breweries. Among names familiar today are: Bass, Charringtons, Courage, Guinness, Watney, Whitbread and Worthington.

Licensing hours were first introduced in the nineteenth century.

After the First World War, bottled beer became popular and widely available. The twentieth century has been a sorry time for beer drinkers. Breweries have combined, stopped producing local brews of character and distinction and brewed bland, nondescript beers designed to appeal to everyone. Many recipes have been discontinued and lots of highly individual, special brews have disappeared.

So that brewers could save on production costs, counter rising taxation, and increase profit margins, the alcohol content of ale and beer, always high in the past, has plummeted.

The strongest draught beers commercially available to us are about 4.5% alcohol by volume (8% proof).

The average commercial beer is about 3.5% alcohol by volume (6% proof).

Compare alcohol levels of some popular mid-nineteenth century brews with our nearest commercial equivalent:

	Nineteenth century	*Today*
Stout	14% alcohol by volume	
	(24.5% proof)	about 4.5% (8% proof)

Old Ale	10.5% by volume	
	(18.5% proof)	about 5% (9% proof)
Porter	8% alcohol by volume	
	(14% proof)	Not available
Pale Ale	6% alcohol by volume	
	(10.5% proof)	about 4.5% (8% proof)

Quality and strength were combined in nineteenth century brews. Today, most commercial beers have neither.

It is up to us now, to make our own superb quality ale, beer and stout at home and continue the tradition of brewing excellence established by our forefathers.

3

YOUR GOOD HEALTH

Ale, beer, lager and stout are brewed from barley. Other grains are sometimes added to give extra flavour and colour. Hops are used for their bitter flavour and preserving quality.

Traditional country ales were flavoured by honey, herbs, flowers, fruits and spices. The health promoting and healing properties of many of these additives were clearly understood by Anglo-Saxon ale brewers.

Nutritional and medicinal qualities of ingredients are extracted by brewing and passed on in the matured ale or beer. The toast, "to your good health" is a statement of fact when you drink traditional brews!

Here is a list of ingredients recommended in recipes included in this book, together with health-giving and healing properties popularly credited to them through centuries of folk medicine.

Caution

Please note that no claims are made for the healing qualities of any of these ingredients. The list is included for your interest and information only and is not intended as a guide to alternative medicine. If you are unwell, consult your doctor and ask him if it is safe for you to drink home brew while taking any medication he might prescribe. Remember also that drinking to excess can lead to hangovers and ultimately alcoholism.

A list of some of the health promoting and healing characteristics traditionally ascribed by folk medicine to ingredients in recipes included in this book

Barley: The main ingredient in all ales and beers. Barley is extremely nourishing and renowned for its body building and strength giving properties. It is easily digested in liquid form and a valuable source of food for the sick and convalescing.

COUNTRY ALES

Apple: Stimulant and health tonic. Contains vitamins A, B, C. Beneficial in cases of anaemia, poor complexion, skin disorder, arthritis and asthma. Helps reduce emotional tension and headaches.

Balm: Soothing. Calms nerves and relieves headaches, toothache and colds. Aids digestion.

Bay leaves: Tonic. Assist digestion and relieve wind and stomach cramps.

Borage: Tonic. Purifies the blood and heals ulcers in the mouth. Eases catarrh and reduces fevers.

Bran: Nutritious, body building. High in vitamin B. Helps relieve arthritis and rheumatism.

Carraway seeds: Effective in treating colds. Help digestion, ease indigestion and release wind.

Cinnamon: Stimulant. Improves digestion. Remedy in cases of diarrhoea and nausea.

Cloves: Stimulant. Improve digestion and raise body temperature. Mild anaesthetic effect in relief of pain.

Comfrey: Nutritious – contains a substantial supply of protein. Wide medicinal properties; purifies the blood and is beneficial in treatment of skin disorders, anaemia, arthritis, asthma, catarrh, colds, coughs, diarrhoea, internal bruising and pain.

Dandelion: Tonic. Purifies the blood, cleanses the liver and acts as a diuretic and mild laxative. Remedy for skin disorders and anaemia.

Fennel: Rejuvenating. Since Roman times believed to improve eyesight. Remedy for stomach acid, cramps and wind.

Ginger: Stimulant. Cure for colds, sore throats and indigestion.

Honey: Rich in essential nutrients. Calming and rejuvenating. Strengthens heart muscles and valuable in treatment of anaemia, arthritis and rheumatism.

Lemon: Natural antiseptic – cleanses the system of impurities and relieves asthma, colds, coughs, gout, rheumatism and sore throats.

Marjoram: Tonic. Restores lost appetite and aids recovery from coughs, headaches and toothache.

Mint: Soothing. Eases pain and relieves colds and headaches.

Nettles: High in vitamins B and C. Remedy for asthma, colds, bronchial coughs, backache and rheumatism.

Nutmeg: Particularly effective in treating nervous disorders and rheumatism.

Parsley: General tonic. Rich in minerals and vitamins A, B, C. Used to treat a variety of ills, including anaemia, arthritis, catarrh, high blood pressure, dropsy, dyspepsia and rheumatism.

Rosemary: Stimulant and tonic. Remedy for colds, sore throats and nervous conditions. Tones body muscles and strengthens the eyes.

Rue: Stimulant and aid to good health. Beneficial in treatment of stomach troubles, headaches, sciatica and gout.

Thyme: Tonic and antiseptic. Helps cure colds, coughs and headaches. Assists digestion and eases asthma.

Woodruff: Stimulant and tonic. Uplifting, restorative effect. Cleanses the liver.

MODERN ALES AND BEERS
Barley: See above.

Hops: Natural antiseptic. Cleanse the liver and purify the blood. Relieve earache and toothache. Sleep inducing.

Maize: Nutritious, body building food. Contains vitamins A, B, C.

Rice: Nourishing and body building. Beneficial for stomach disorders and relief of diarrohea.

If you have not already done so, please refer to the *Caution* at the beginning of this list.

4

COMMERCIAL BREWING

Breweries use a lengthy and complex process to produce beer. Home brewing is simple by comparison. But commercial methods are worth examining.

Technical terms, the jargon loved and habitually used by some home brewers, are bracketed next to the items and procedure they describe.

Ale and beer begin life as barley grains, soaked in water for two to four days. The water is then drained and the barley left for five days at a temperature of 16° C (58° – 60° F) to germinate (malting).

During this period a natural chemical reaction in the barley turns its starch into fermentable sugar (maltose). Nutrients, which nourish and encourage the beer yeast's fermentation of sugar also develop. Tiny shoots show from the dried barley at the end of this stage. These are removed and the barley is cured by further heating (kilning) before being used for brewing.

The final colour of a brew is decided by the temperature at which the barley is heated (kilned). A high temperature results in a darker colour and subtle difference in flavour. Caramel is sometimes used to colour a brew. Any addition of cereals like maize or rice also affects colour and flavour.

Next, the barley is ground (cracked), mixed with hot water (liquour) and kept at a constant temperature of 62°–68°C (145°–155°F). When extraction of flavour and goodness (mashing) is complete the liquid (wort) is filtered from the barley which is rinsed (sparged) with hot water or liquid (wort) to make sure everything of value to the finished beer has been removed. The barley grains (grist) are discarded and sold as animal feed.

The liquid (wort) is boiled with hops for two or three hours to acquire their flavour, bitterness and aroma. Some hops are added towards the end of this process (dry hopping). Hops are then strained off and sold as fertilizer.

The natural sugar (maltose) content of the liquid (wort) is measured and sufficient processed cane and beet sugar (sucrose) may be added to raise the combined sugar content of the liquid (wort) to the amount necessary to produce the desired level of alcohol.

Next, beer yeast is placed (pitched) in the liquid (wort) which is often fermented to non-sweetness (dryness) in a day or two. During fermentation frothing surface beer yeast is skimmed off occasionally.

Natural, "real" ale and beer is casked just before fermentation is complete and beer yeast present in the unfiltered (living) beer finishes fermentation in the cask, giving the brew its natural life and sparkle.

Keg, bottled and canned ales and beers are filtered and all beer yeast destroyed. Their sparkle is due to the artificial injection of carbon dioxide gas (carbonation).

5

WHAT BREWS HOME BEER?

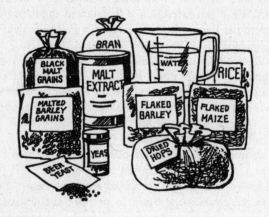

All types of ale and beer are brewed from four basic ingredients:
1 **Barley malt**
2 **Hops, or alternative natural flavouring**
3 **Water**
4 **Beer yeast**

1. Barley malt

Barley grain, properly germinated and dried is called malted barley grain. Crushed and then boiled in water, it provides flavour, nourishment and natural sugar (maltose) for brewing. Beer yeast turns sugar into alcohol during fermentation.

You can buy barley grains ready malted and cut out the tiresome task of germinating and drying the grain. Malted barley grains need only crushing and boiling.

The easiest way to make superb home brew is to *buy pure malt extract* from your local health or homebrew stockist. This saves you crushing large quantities of grain and reduces the need for boiling to a minimum.

Recipes in this book use pure malt extract and small amounts of grain to achieve brews of excellent quality.

Pure malt extract, designed for home brewing, is available as syrup or powder. The powder is easier to handle but must be stored in a dry place if not required immediately. Syrup should be kept somewhere cool.

Buy *unhopped* pure malt extract and look out for special types prepared for particular styles of beer. Any pure malt may be used but superior brews result from using dark malts to make strong bitter, brown ale and stout and light malts for ale, light bitter and lager.

Pure malt extract is sold in containers ranging in size from 2 lbs (907 gms) to 56 lbs (25½ kgs) in weight. You can economise by buying in bulk, but aim to use it within a few months of purchase.

The quantity of pure malt used in a brew affects the fullness, flavour and alcohol level of your beer.

Your brew will be improved by adding some cereal grains. Here is a list of adjuncts recommended in this book. Full instructions for their preparation and use are included in recipes.

ADJUNCT	BENEFICIAL EFFECT
Black malt grains	distinctive colour and flavour
Bran	increased body and texture
Crystal malt grains	improved colour and body
Flaked barley	extra flavour and body
Flaked maize	enhanced flavour and texture
Rice	fuller, rounder texture and body

All these ingredients are stocked by health and homebrew shops.

2. Hops

Add bitterness to beer and help it keep longer.

Several varieties exist.

Fuggles and Goldings are most commonly used for brewing ale, beer and stout.

Hallertau give a more delicate flavour to lager.

Dried hops, ideal for home brewing, are readily available from health and homebrew shops.

3. Water

Hard water is generally preferred for brewing light ale and bitter beer.

Soft water is favoured for mild ale and stout.

If you do not mind putting chemicals in your brew, you can adjust water for special results by adding:

Epsom salts (magnesium sulphate) to harden water.

Salt (sodium chloride) to soften water and round the brew's flavour.

Directions for the optional addition of Epsom salts or salt are given in recipes.

4. Beer yeast

Beer yeast (saccharomyces cerevisiae) is available as dried granules in single packets or tubs and as a liquid, natural culture in a phial.

It ferments rapidly on the surface of your brew and converts natural sugar (maltose) and any added household sugar (sucrose) to alcohol.

Beer yeast works best at a temperature of about 18°C (64°F) and imparts extra flavour to your brew.

Lager yeast (saccharomyces carlsbergensis) ferments from the bottom of your brew; lends a unique taste to lager and is marketed in the same way as beer yeast.

6

SUGAR-FREE BREWING

Traditional English country ales and beers relied on beer yeast fermenting the natural sugar (maltose) found in malted barley grains to provide the alcohol content of a brew. These ales and beers were of exceptionally high quality; full flavoured, strong and nourishing.

Processed cane and beet sugar (sucrose) was not widely employed by British commercial brewers to ferment alcohol until the late nineteenth century. The main attraction of cane sugar for brewers was its cheapness compared with pure malt. By replacing some of the malt with processed cane and beet sugar (sucrose), brewers were able to maintain the level of alcohol in a brew while considerably reducing the malt required to supply natural malt sugar (maltose) and cut production costs. This practice was loudly criticised by drinkers at the time but to no effect. As a result commercial ale and beer has become steadily more bland and insipid.

German law forbids inclusion of processed sugar (sucrose) in a brew and refuses to recognise beer not brewed wholly from malt.

About 75% of pure malt extract syrup is fermentable natural sugar (maltose). Dried pure malt extract powder consists mainly of natural sugar (maltose).

Recipes in this book offer you the opportunity to brew true ale, beer, lager and stout in the finest Anglo-Saxon tradition by making use of the natural sugar (maltose) present in pure malt to ferment alcohol. Malt only brews are high quality, delicious and nutritious.

7

MONEY-SAVING BREWS

You may like to make especially economical, quality brews by replacing some pure malt extract with granulated household sugar (sucrose).

Recipes in this book give clear instructions to enable you to produce first class, money-saving ales, beers, lagers and stout using pure malt and a minimum of granulated household sugar (sucrose).

Your economy brews will have a lighter colour, taste and texture than traditional whole malt brews.

For a little extra money you can change the flavour, body and "feel" of each of your economy brews by replacing any measure of granulated household sugar with an equal amount of brown sugar, demerara sugar, golden syrup or pure honey. You may replace all the granulated sugar, if you wish.

To help with your adventurous economy brewing, here is a table describing the influence these pure malt substitutes are likely to have on your finished brew.

PURE MALT SUBSTITUTE	INFLUENCE ON BREW
Brown sugar	Subtle deepening of colour, texture and flavour.
Demerara sugar	Strong, rich golden colour, flavour and body.
Golden syrup	Smooth texture and taste.
Granulated sugar	Neutral – emphasises the natural malt and hop or alternative flavouring of the brew. Otherwise, no discernible effect, except that it tends to reduce the fullness of the flavour.

Pure honey   Full, round, rich flavour and silky "feel".
     Endless permutations of blends are possible and it is rewarding to experiment and develop secret recipes and special brews.

8

EQUIPMENT

You do not need a lot of equipment to start brewing. Visit your local homebrew stockist and browse through the items on display. It is a good idea to get to know what is available. The specialist staff are always willing to advise and help.

Bucket or brewing bin with lid

What you require depends on how much beer you intend making. One gallon (4½ litres) fills eight one pint (½ litre) bottles. This amount is easily brewed in a two gallon plastic *food grade* bucket. A headspace of 2 – 4 inches (51 mm – 102 mm) should be allowed for frothing during fermentation.

Larger quantities of beer are best brewed in a 3¼ gallon (15 litre) or 5½ gallon (25 litre) plastic brewing bin. These are sold with lids. You need a well fitting (but not airtight) lid or covering for your bucket or bin to keep out insects, dust and airborne bacteria. A large square of clean material fastened with string is adequate.

Metal containers are NOT suitable for fermenting beer because the alcohol produced can absorb mildly poisonous chemicals from the metal.

Saucepans with lids

One or two large saucepans capable of holding 7–8 pints (4–4½ litres) of liquid are desirable, together with lids. One large saucepan will suffice if you are brewing one gallon (4½ litres) of beer at a time. You may use several smaller saucepans instead, if you wish.

Syphon tubing

Plastic syphon tubing about 4–5 feet (1.2–1.5 metres) in length is always useful and a small plastic on/off tap can be bought to fit standard size plastic tubing. It is wise to invest in such a tap.

Polythene funnel

A polythene funnel with a mouth 4–6 inches (102 mm–152 mm) in diameter is worth having.

Strainer

A finely meshed nylon sieve, or suitable strainer is an important piece of equipment.

Kitchen scales

You probably already have these. A set of kitchen scales is necessary for accurate measurement of ingredients.

Measuring jug

A calibrated measuring jug helps keep an accurate account of ingredients included in your brew.

To bottle or not to bottle . . .

You can choose to bottle or to barrel your beer. There are advantages in both methods.

Bottling

Brews mature quickly in beer bottles and remain in excellent sparkling condition for many months. Beer bottles can be stored in convenient places and easily moved to new locations. They are easily chilled in a fridge; may be offered as gifts, or taken on picnics or to parties. However, bottling beer takes longer than barrelling it.

Barrelling

Barrelling beer in plastic pressure barrels, specially designed for home brews, is quick and easy. The beer is draught in character and drawing your own pint from a pressure barrel is a satisfying and rewarding experience. A pressure barrel is particularly useful when holding a party and saves collecting and rinsing empty beer bottles. The disadvantages are that barrelled beers take slightly longer to clear and mature; do not keep their condition for more than a few weeks once several pints have been drawn off and are heavy to move, requiring a semi-permanent resting place.

A happy medium

Many home brewers bottle strong and special brews and barrel lighter, less costly ones intended for regular consumption.

Bottles

Buy 1 pint (½ litre) beer bottles *specially designed* for your home brewed beer from your local homebrew stockist.

Some home brewers bottle beer in screw-top lemonade or cider bottles, or ordinary non-returnable commercial beer bottles bought from an off-licence. Such bottles will not withstand the pressure of carbon dioxide gas formed naturally in your beer after it has been bottled. Bottles not manufactured for home brew are likely to explode and can cause *serious* injury – **NEVER USE THEM**.

Bottle caps

Metal caps to fit 1 pint (½ litre) home brew beer bottles are also stocked by homebrew specialists.

Capping tool

You need a capping tool to crimp the edges of the metal caps securely around the mouth of your bottles and guarantee an air-tight seal.

Several designs of capping tool are commercially available, ranging from inexpensive hand held capping tools – which are gently tapped with a hammer to fasten the metal caps in place, to more sophisticated lever action models.

Pressure barrels

When barrelling brews use only specially designed *plastic pressure barrels*. Wooden barrels are difficult to keep clean and sterilise satisfactorily, admit too much air and generally fail to keep the brew in tip top condition.

There are many designs of plastic pressure barrel for you to choose from, in sizes holding from 2½ gallons (11½ litres) to 5 gallons (23 litres).

As you drink your barrelled beer, so its natural sparkle and condition fades. Towards the end of the barrelled brew you can recondition the beer by injecting carbon dioxide gas into it with an *injector unit*. These small units screw into the tops of pressure barrels and are usually sold as optional extras, complete with operating instructions.

Bottle brush

A wire handled bottle brush is invaluable for reaching into awkward corners when cleaning bottles and barrels.

9

HOME BREWING

Cleanliness

Never risk bacterial infection and spoilage of your brew. Before brewing, clean equipment with warm water. Use a bottle brush for reaching into awkward corners. Then sterilise ALL your equipment by rinsing with sulphite solution (see below). This kills bacteria.

Sulphite solution

This solution is made by mixing sodium metabisulphite with water. Sodium metabisulphite is available from your chemist or homebrew shop as powder – ½ lb (227 gms) is a handy quantity, or in the more expensive form of Campden tablets.

Dissolve 1 oz (28 gms) of sodium metabisulphite powder or 9 crushed Campden tablets in 1 pint (½ litre) of warm water.

Do not breathe the fumes given off when the chemical mixes with water as these can cause momentary irritation to your nose, throat and lungs.

Store sulphite solution in a cork-stoppered bottle. After being used to rinse equipment, it can be poured back into the bottle. In this way, it may be used repeatedly and remains potent for months.

Always remove traces of the solution from equipment before brewing by rinsing with warm water.

After use make sure equipment is thoroughly cleaned and dried before being packed away.

Brewing

Pure malt extract is used for brewing all recipes in this book, cutting out the long, tedious business of malting and temperature controlled mashing of barley grain. A small measure of fresh grain is added to increase quality, bite and flavour.

Beer yeast

All types of beer yeast will activate automatically when added directly to your brew, but for best results always follow the manufacturer's instructions.

Starter bottle

By making a starter bottle of activated beer yeast before beginning to prepare your brew, you guarantee a rapid start and faster finish to its fermentation.

METHOD

1. Activate beer yeast

Activate the beer yeast in your starter bottle by pouring the quantity of beer yeast suggested in the manufacturer's instructions through a sterilised, rinsed polythene funnel into a sterilised, rinsed one pint ($\frac{1}{2}$ litre) bottle. Dissolve 1 heaped tablespoon of pure malt extract syrup OR 1 level tablespoon of dried malt extract powder in $\frac{1}{4}$ pint (142 mls) of hot water (malt extract supplies natural sugar – maltose – and essential nutrients to nourish the beer yeast). Cover and allow to cool. When cool, pour into the bottle and add 1 level (5 ml) teaspoon of pure lemon juice (to speed initial fermentation of beer yeast in the starter bottle). Then three-quarters fill the bottle with warm – not boiling – water. Loosely cover the top of the bottle with a 4 inch (102 mm) square of sterilised, rinsed polythene, or silver cooking foil, secured around the bottle neck by an elastic band and put it aside while you prepare equipment and ingredients. Most types of beer yeast will normally be active, frothing and ready for use in approximately an hour. Some types of beer yeast take longer. Check any instructions that come with your beer yeast for precise details.

2. Assemble equipment

Next, assemble your equipment:

a) *Bucket or brewing bin with lid*
b) *Saucepans with lids*
c) *Strainer*
d) *Kitchen scales*
e) *Measuring jug*
f) *Large spoon for stirring*

Clean all equipment and sterilise with sulphite solution (sodium metabisulphite mixed with water, see page 32). Pour the solution back into its storage bottle and fasten cork stopper. Rinse your equipment with warm water to remove traces of sulphite solution.
*TIP

Fast fermentation and clearing

To encourage rapid fermentation and quick clearing of your brew by natural means, a small measure of brewed tea (tannin) and pure lemon juice (citric acid) is included in each recipe.

3. Assemble ingredients
a) Pure malt extract
b) Hops or alternative natural flavouring
c) Any grain additives
d) Sugar (sucrose) IF BEING USED
e) Epsom salts (magnesium sulphate) or salt (sodium chloride) IF BEING USED
f) Tea and fresh lemon

4. Make tea. Extract lemon juice
a) Make tea and allow to cool, or use leftover tea from an earlier pot
b) Extract juice from lemon
*TIP

Lemon juice

Remove small quantities of pure lemon juice by pricking the lemon through its skin with a sterilised, rinsed needle and squeezing out the required amount. The lemon reseals itself and may be kept fresh stored in your fridge.

5. Simmer about 5-6 pints (3-3½ litres) of water in large saucepan
a) Add pure malt extract; ½ total quantity hops or alternative natural flavouring and any other ingredients, as directed in recipes.
b) Stir until malt extract is dissolved.
c) HOME BREWERS USING HOUSEHOLD SUGAR (SUCROSE) OR GOLDEN SYRUP. Stir in the required amount until dissolved.
d) Cover with lid and simmer gently for 15 minutes.

e) Add remaining ½ of hops or alternative natural flavouring and any pure honey being used. Cover and simmer for 10 minutes. Then switch off heat and allow to cool.

*TIP

Pure malt extract syrup

Soak jars or tins of pure malt extract syrup in a bowl of warm water for a few minutes to loosen it for easier pouring before brewing.

6. When liquid is cool

a) When cool, pour the liquid from your saucepan or saucepans through a sterilised, rinsed nylon sieve or suitable strainer into a sterilised, rinsed plastic (food grade) bucket or brewing bin. If you find the saucepan too heavy to lift safely, scoop up the liquid in your measuring jug and strain it into your bucket or bin in easy stages.

b) Discard hops and all other solid additives. If you have a garden, they make excellent compost.

c) Pour in activated beer yeast from starter bottle.

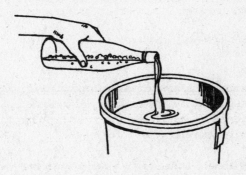

d) Add strained cold tea and pure lemon juice.

e) Add cold water to bring the total liquid in your bucket or brewing bin to the quantity of beer required.

f) Allow at least 2 inches (51 mm) – 4 inches (102 mm) head space at the top of your bucket or bin for frothing and foaming. Cover.

g) Remove somewhere warm to finish fermenting. A temperature of about 18°C (64°F) is ideal.

7. Judging when fermentation has finished

Fermentation has finished when your brew has fermented to dryness (non-sweetness). Dryness is reached when all natural sugar in the malt (maltose) and any additional processed household sugar (sucrose) has been converted to alcohol by the beer yeast.

Signs to look for

Fermentation has ceased when bubbling and frothing has stopped; the surface is still, beginning to clear and the brew tastes dry (non-sweet) and is not fizzy on your tongue.

The warmer the temperature, the sooner a brew ferments to dryness. At a temperature of about 18°C (64°F) fermentation usually takes from 6–14 days to finish. Brews strong in alcohol can take longer to finish fermenting than brews relatively low in alcohol. Recipes in this book give you an idea of when to expect your beer to finish fermenting.

When fermentation is completed, your brew is ready for bottling or barrelling.

10

BOTTLING, BARRELLING AND STORAGE

When you are satisfied that fermentation has finished (see page 36) the time has come to bottle or barrel your brew. **WARNING** – when bottling your brew, use only the beer bottles specially designed for home brew, available from your local homebrew stockist. Other bottles *may explode* and can cause serious injury.

METHOD
1. Sterilise equipment
Clean, sterilise with sulphite solution (sodium metabisulphite mixed with water, see page 32) and then rinse with warm water:
a) Home brew beer bottles or plastic pressure barrel
b) Home brew beer bottle caps
c) Syphon tubing
d) Polythene funnel

2. Prime your brew
To give your brew sparkle and life in bottles or barrel and keep it in good condition, you must prime it. Priming is achieved by adding natural sugar (maltose) found in pure malt extract, or granulated household sugar (sucrose) to your brew immediately before bottling or barrelling. The pure malt extract or granulated sugar is fermented in the bottles or barrel by beer yeast remaining in the clearing brew and this second minor fermentation produces a protective blanket of carbon dioxide gas naturally, giving the brew sparkling, lively appeal and protecting it against bacterial infection.

To prime your brew:

a) Pour two or three cupfuls of your brew into a sterilised, rinsed saucepan and gently heat until simmering. Then stir in and dissolve 2 level tablespoons of pure malt extract syrup (maltose) OR 1½ level tablespoons of pure malt extract dried powder (maltose) OR 1½ level tablespoons of granulated household sugar (sucrose) for each gallon (4½ litres) of brew you wish to prime. Cover and allow to cool. **WARNING** – Never exceed the recommended measure of pure malt extract or granulated sugar, or your bottles may explode!

b) When cool, pour the sweetened priming beer from the saucepan into the bucket or brewing bin holding your fermented brew. Stir two or three times, taking care not to disturb too much the thick layer of beer yeast at the bottom of your bucket or bin. Cover and leave for about ten minutes to blend and mix thoroughly.

3. Filling bottles and barrels

a) After allowing sufficient time for the dissolved pure malt extract or granulated sugar to permeate your brew, rest the bucket or brewing bin on a strong, solid surface at a higher level than the bottles or barrel to be filled.

b) If your tube is not long enough to reach, then place the polythene funnel in the neck of your barrel or first beer bottle.

c) Put one end of your syphon tubing in the bucket or brewing bin containing your brew so it rests just above the bed of beer yeast at

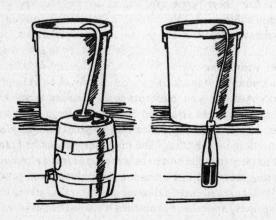

the bottom of the bucket or bin; suck beer into the syphon tube and hold the other end in the mouth of your funnel. Beer will flow through the tube into your bottle or barrel provided that the end of the tube outside the brew is kept at a lower level than the surface of the brew in the bin.

Filling beer bottles

Fill beer bottles to within 1 inch (25 mm) of the top of each bottle. Then stop the flow of beer through the syphon tube by pinching the end and raising it level with the top of your bucket or brewing bin. If you have invested in a small plastic on/off tap, simply switch off the flow of beer. Then fill the next bottle.

Filling plastic pressure barrels

Fill your plastic pressure barrel to its shoulder, allowing 2–3 inches (51–76 mm) air space between its cap and the surface of your brew.

*TIP

Beer yeast

After your first purchase of beer yeast, if you intend to brew regularly, you need never buy any more. Just follow these instructions:

a) Remove two heaped tablespoons of beer yeast from the bottom of your bucket or brewing bin after bottling or barrelling your brew. The beer yeast will ferment another brew and stored in a covered sterilised, rinsed cup or jar keeps fresh in a fridge for a week, or wrapped in a sheet of sterilised, rinsed polythene in a freezer for up to six months. Whichever method you choose, activate the beer yeast before use in a starter bottle by adding warm water, pure malt extract and pure lemon juice as described on page 33. When it is fermenting and frothing it is ready to pour into your brew and will ferment up to 5½ gallons (25 litres) of beer.

OR

b) Pour a fresh brew directly onto the bed of beer yeast in your bucket or brewing bin after bottling or barrelling. Fermentation starts almost immediately. When brewing continuously in this fashion, occasionally remove some of the beer yeast or eventually it will fill the container. If the bed of beer yeast starts to look littered with the residue of hops and grain, or smells unpleasant, throw it away.

4. Capping

a) Beer bottles

When you have filled your beer bottles, firmly fasten the special

caps with your capping tool.

b) Pressure barrels

Simply screw the cap on tightly.

*TIP

Moving heavy bins and barrels

Five gallons (23 litres) of beer weighs about 50 lbs (23 kgs). Easier moving is achieved by using a trolley.

A trolley is easily made by screwing four castors to a thick wooden board.

5. Storage

a) Wipe clean, clearly label and store your bottled or barrelled brew somewhere fairly warm, about 18°C (64°F) for 7 days, to encourage fermentation of priming malt (maltose) or granulated sugar (sucrose), and formation of carbon dioxide gas.

b) After 7 days move your bottles or barrel to a cooler place, about 10°C (50°F) for 4–5 weeks to help it clear. All brews will clear naturally, assisted by the addition during brewing of tea (tannin) and pure lemon juice (citric acid) as detailed in recipes.

For the best development of your brew's fullness and flavour store it somewhere cool, round 10°C (50°F) to 13°C (55°F) and away from direct sunlight.

6. Ready to drink

Recipes give you an idea of when to expect your brew to be ready for enjoyable drinking.

Your home brew should maintain its high quality for several months after being bottled or barrelled and high alcohol brews often remain in superb condition for up to a year – if you can bear to leave them that long.

11

CHEMICAL-FREE BREWS

All sorts of chemical aids are commercially available to home brewers. They include such items as crystals to adjust tap water for brewing ale; vitamin tablets to hurry fermentation and beer finings to clear brews before being bottled or barrelled. You may choose to experiment with these, but by using pure, natural ingredients it is possible to brew excellent ale, beer, lager and stout without adding chemicals to your brew, as our ancestors did.

Sodium metabisulphite

Mixed with water (see page 32) sodium metabisulphite makes an effective sterilising agent called *sulphite solution* that destroys bacteria on equipment and prevents possible infection of your brew. It is advisable to sterilise all your equipment with sulphite solution before brewing. But make sure you *rinse away* all traces of the solution with warm water before using items of equipment.

Epsom salts

A ¼ teaspoon of Epsom salts (magnesium sulphate) can be used to harden one gallon (4½ litres) of tap water for brewing light ales and bitter beers, but its use is entirely optional.

Salt

Up to ½ level (5 ml) teaspoon of salt (sodium chloride) may be added to soften one gallon (4½ litres) of tap water when brewing mild ale and stout. Its use is, however, a matter of choice.

Full instructions for the optional use of Epsom salts and salt are included in appropriate recipes.

12

WHAT GOES WRONG
WITH BEER

Not a lot.

Beer is simple to make and little can go wrong.

But here is a list of things unlikely to happen, but which might, just to try your patience.

Burst beer bottles:

Naughty!

You have either:

a) Bottled too soon, before fermentation finished.

b) Primed with too much pure malt extract (maltose) or granulated sugar (sucrose).

c) Used chipped or cracked home brew beer bottles.

d) Collected bottles not designed for home brew and unsuitable for holding beer under pressure (see page 30).

Remedy:

Work out what went wrong and take precautions to prevent it happening again. Bursting bottles can cause serious injury and always create mess.

Flatness:

Your beer has no sparkle. Not the end of the world. If you followed the recipe it tastes good.

You have either:

a) Forgotten to prime your brew with pure malt extract (maltose) or granulated sugar (sucrose).

b) Used beer bottles chipped at the mouth, or improperly sealed.

Remedy:

Bottled beer

a) Replace any beer bottles with chipped mouths.

b) Reprime each one pint ($\frac{1}{2}$ litre) bottle of flat beer with a heaped teaspoon (5 mls) of pure malt extract syrup (maltose) **OR** a level teaspoon (5 mls) of pure malt extract dried powder (maltose) **OR** a level teaspoon (5 mls) of granulated sugar (sucrose). Dissolve the pure malt extract or granulated sugar in a small amount of the bottled brew warmed in a sterilised, rinsed saucepan. Remember to keep the bottle covered while you are doing this. Cover the saucepan and allow the primed brew to cool before pouring it back into the bottle through a sterilised, rinsed polythene funnel.

c) Re-cap the bottle. It is advisable to use a new cap.

d) Check caps on other bottles for cracks. Replace any damaged ones after repriming the flat brew.

e) Listen for the hiss of escaping carbon dioxide gas from leaking caps and fasten them securely. Replace where necessary.

Barrelled beer

a) Reprime your flat brew by dissolving 2 level tablespoons of pure malt extract syrup (maltose) or $1\frac{1}{2}$ level tablespoons of pure malt extract dried powder (maltose) or $1\frac{1}{2}$ level tablespoons of granulated sugar (sucrose) for each gallon ($4\frac{1}{2}$ litres) of barrelled beer in a few cupfuls of the flat brew, warmed in a sterilised, rinsed saucepan. Cover and allow to cool. When cool, pour the reprimed beer back into your plastic pressure barrel and screw the cap on securely.

b) Check your barrel cap is properly screwed down. You can put a sterilised, rinsed square of polythene inside the cap for a better seal. It may need a new rubber sealing ring. These are stocked by homebrew specialists.

No head on poured beer:

Either the brew is flat (see Flatness), or you have traces of detergent or grease in your tankard or glass inhibiting head formation and retention.

Remedy:

Wash tankard or glass in warm water and detergent. Rinse thoroughly with cold water. Pour yourself another pint. Cheers!

Foaming and frothing of poured beer:

The beer settles, given time.

You have either:

a) Primed with too much pure malt extract (maltose) or granulated sugar (sucrose).

b) Bottled or barrelled before fermentation ceased.

Remedy:

Overcome this annoying hindrance to quaffing your brew by storing beer bottles in a cool place. Chill before serving. Barrels sort themselves out after a few pints have been drawn off.

Check to make sure you left 1 inch (25 mm) air space between bottle cap and beer to accommodate carbon dioxide gas, or filled your barrel only to its shoulder. If you did not leave this minimum space, never mind. Remember next time.

Tastes peculiar:

Your brew may be infected by bacteria because the bottle or barrel was not sterilised with sulphite solution and rinsed with water before being filled. It is also possible that not all the sulphite solution was rinsed away with water and your beer's flavour is tainted.

Decide for yourself whether to throw away your brew or chalk it down to experience and drink up regardless.

13

SERVING BEER

Let your beer mature for at least the minimum time suggested in the recipe.

Wash glasses or tankards in detergent to remove any grease spots, which can prevent an attractive head forming.

Rinse away detergent with cold water to cool your drinking vessel.

Dry only the outside of the glass or tankard, in case bits of cloth stick to the inside.

Flick out droplets of water.

Pewter tankards keep beer cool, enhancing its taste.

Traditional pewter tankards often have a glass bottom so that you can see what your companions are up to when it is fully raised!

Solid based tankards create a blind spot when held to the lips and in the good old days the drinker was, at this moment, vulnerable to attack – hence the glass bottom.

A straight glass or glass mug gives paranoid drinkers all round vision and allows enjoyment of the beer's colour and bubbly effervescence.

Serve light ales and lager chilled, to crisp their tangy flavour.

Other ales, bitter and stout taste best cool, not cold.

Open bottles carefully and steadily to avoid disturbing sediment.

Reduce frothing by pouring beer gently along the inside of your tankard or glass.

Keep the bottle at an angle and stop pouring when dregs appear. Store dregs in a large lightly stoppered sterilised, rinsed bottle for cooking.

In the summer enjoy long, thirst quenching draughts of chilled light ale and lager.

Winter beers should be strong, full bodied, nourishing and warming.

Stout makes an excellent nightcap, as does mulled or heated spiced ale.

Beware of quaffing strong home brew by the pint. Remember its potency is greater than that of commercial beer.

Drink high alcohol beers by the half pint.

Recipes give you an idea of alcohol content.

Very strong beer can be sipped from a brandy glass.

All ales and beers go well with crusty wholemeal rolls and cheese or salad.

Light ale and lager complement curries, highly spiced food, fish and white meat dishes.

Strong ale and bitter beer taste best with red meat dishes or fish and chips.

14

BEER COOKERY

Terrific tastes and fabulous flavours are bestowed on ordinary dishes by using ale, beer or lager in exactly the same way cordon bleu chefs use wine.

Try some of these dishes and then move on to devise your own exciting, mouth-watering recipes.

For best results use ingredients uncontaminated by chemical additives.

Ale cake
Ingredients
Ale or beer – ¼ pint (142 mls)
Currants – 12 oz (340 gms)
Free range eggs – 2
Wholemeal flour – 8 oz (227 gms)
Soft vegetable margarine – 4 oz (113 gms)
Ground mixed spice – ¼ teaspoon
Pure honey – 2 level tablespoons
Method
Mix together margarine, honey, eggs and ale or beer. Mix in all other ingredients until well blended. Put into greased cake tin and bake in moderate oven, gas no. 4 (350° F) for about 1½ hours. After removing cake tin from oven, leave cake in tin for ten minutes; then turn out onto cooling rack. When cold, store in air-tight container for 24 hours before cutting.

Brown onion soup
Ingredients – serves 4
Bitter beer – ½ pint (284 mls)

Lean bacon – 1 slice, chopped
Wholemeal bread roll, or slice of stale wholemeal bread – 1
Soft vegetable margarine – 2 oz (56 gms)
Onions – 1½ lbs (680 gms), chopped
Freshly ground black pepper – to taste
Vegetable stock (liquid collected from cooked vegetables) – ½ pint
  (284 mls)
Method

Melt margarine in pan. Add chopped onions and fry until well browned. Cover and cook on a slow heat for 30 minutes. Add stock, beer, chopped bacon and bread broken in pieces. Pepper to taste. Cover and simmer for about 1 hour. Then rub through a sieve and serve with cheese croûtons or toast cut into small squares.

Casserole of beef
Ingredients – serves 4
Ale or beer – ½ pint (284 mls)
Bay leaves – 2
Carrots – ½ lb (227 gms), sliced
Pure vegetable oil – sufficient for frying
Wholemeal flour – 1 oz (28 gms)
Onions – ½ lb (227 gms), chopped
Sea salt and freshly ground black pepper – to taste
Stewing steak – 1 lb (½ kg)
Method

Season meat with salt and pepper and coat with flour. Fry in oil with chopped onions. Put in casserole with sliced carrots and bay leaves. Cover with ale or beer and cook in slow oven, gas no. 2 (300° F) for about 1½ hours. Remove bay leaves. Serve with boiled potatoes.

Cheesey smoked haddock
Ingredients – serves 2
Bitter beer – ½ pint (284 mls)
Grated cheese – 4 oz (113 gms)
Wholewheat flour – 1 oz (28 gms)
Milk – ¼ pint (142 mls)
English mustard powder – ¼ teaspoon
Smoked fillets of haddock – 2

Method

Wash and dry fish and poach for 10–15 minutes in beer. Remove fish from pan and put in oven proof dish. Make cheese sauce by mixing flour, milk, cheese and mustard over low heat till thick. Pour over fish and brown for about 15 minutes in hot oven, gas no. 6 (400°F) or under grill. Serve on mashed potato.

Chicken soup

Ingredients – serves 4–5

Lager or light ale – ½ pint (284 mls)

Carrot – 1 medium size

Minced chicken – 2 heaped tablespoons

Turnip – 1

Fresh parsley – 1 sprig

  or dried – ¼ teaspoon

Fresh thyme – 1 sprig

  or dried – ¼ teaspoon

Stock, made from chicken bones and trimmings – 1 pint (½ litre)

Method

Prepare and slice vegetables. Put into stewpan with stock and other ingredients. Bring to boiling point and simmer for 30 minutes, or until tender. Then serve.

*TIP

Fritters

Use ale or beer in place of milk when making fritter batter – no eggs required.

Goulash

Ingredients – serves 2

Ale – ½ pint (284 mls)

Bouquet garni

Sliced carrots – 2

Wholemeal flour – 1 oz (28 gms)

Pure vegetable oil – sufficient for frying

Sliced onions – ½ lb (227 gms)

Sliced parsnip – 1 medium size

Sea salt and freshly ground black pepper – to your taste

Stewing beef – 1 lb (½ kg)

Stock (stock cube) – ¼ pint (142 mls)

Method

Brown prepared vegetables by frying in oil. Cut meat into pieces and roll them in flour seasoned with salt and pepper. Add meat to vegetables and brown. Pour in ale. Let it reduce a little. Sprinkle any remaining flour over meat. Put in oven proof casserole dish. Add enough stock to cover and the bouquet garni. Cover with lid and cook in a slow oven, gas no. 3 (325° F) for about 2 hours. Then serve.

Lamb stew

Ingredients – serves 4

Lager – ¼ pint (142 mls)
Carrots – 1 lb (½ kg)
Dried mixed herbs – 1 level teaspoon
Neck of lamb – 2 lbs (1 kg)
Onions – 2
Sea salt and freshly ground black pepper – to your taste

Method

Cut meat into small joints and slice vegetables. Arrange in layers in an oven proof casserole dish. Sprinkle on mixed herbs, salt and pepper, to taste. Add lager. Cook in a slow oven, gas no. 3 (325° F) for about 2 hours. Serve with large potatoes, scrubbed and baked in their jackets. These can be cooked in the oven on a baking tray at the same time as the casserole.

*TIP

Sausages

Poach sausages in beer before adding them to batter for toad in the hole.

*TIP

Welsh rarebit

Add a tablespoon of bitter beer when making welsh rarebit and a dash of Worcester sauce.

15

MAKE MALT VINEGAR

Making your own malt vinegar is easy.

Try using vinegar made from home brewed honey, herb, flower and fruit ales as healthy and appetizing alternatives to commercial-style malt vinegar.

Vinegar improves salad dressings and marinades; tenderises meat and uniquely flavours cooked dishes and natural foods.

Wait until the ale or beer of your choice finishes fermenting, remove the quantity you wish to turn into vinegar and dilute each pint (½ litre) with ¼ pint (142 mls) of water; add ½ pint (284 mls) of commercial malt vinegar.

Mix well and half fill sterilised, rinsed bottles or a large narrow necked vessel.

Plug with cotton wool and store somewhere warm for about eight weeks.

First a haze forms, then a wrinkled surface skin develops. When transformation into vinegar is complete, the liquid is clear.

When clear and bright, syphon the vinegar off its sediment and fill clean, sterilised and rinsed bottles to within 2¼ inches (57 mm) of the top of the bottle. Lightly stopper, or plug bottles with cotton wool and pasteurise the vinegar by standing the bottles on a cloth, wooden board or folded newspaper in a large saucepan of hot – not boiling – water. Maintain heat *below* boiling for thirty minutes. Then carefully remove bottles and fasten sterilised, rinsed cork or plastic stoppers.

Label and store for two months to mature.

Keep well away from stocks of beer to prevent absorption of vinegar odour.

Sterilise and rinse all equipment used.

16

ALE CUPS

Winter cups

In the freezing, dark winter days before central heating and electric lights, our ancestors warmed themselves with a tankard of hot ale or beer laced with health promoting herbs and spices to keep away colds and influenza – and it really does work. Try for yourself and see.

*Adjust the quantity of ingredients in these recipes according to the amount you or your guests wish to drink.

Winter punch

This once popular English tonic glows with nourishment and powerful vitamins.

Ingredients: To make 1¼ pints (¾ litre)

Ale or beer – 1 pint (½ litre)

Cloves – 3

Ground ginger – 1 level teaspoon

Pure honey – 1 level tablespoon

Pure lemon juice – 1 level tablespoon

Ground mixed spice – ¼ teaspoon

Water – ¼ pint (142 mls)

Method

Place all ingredients in a large saucepan and warm until simmering. Then remove from heat, cover and allow to cool. When cool, reheat until simmering and strain into warmed tankards, glasses or cups and drink while hot. A thin slice of lemon floated on the surface of each drink looks attractive.

Caudle

Very popular pick-me-up in Elizabethan England. Full of flavour and goodness.

Ingredients: To make 1 pint (½ litre)

Ale or beer – 1 pint (½ litre)

Pure honey – 2 heaped tablespoons

Pure lemon juice – 1 level tablespoon

Oatmeal – 1 level tablespoon

Ground nutmeg – ¼ teaspoon

Method

Put all the ingredients in a large saucepan and warm until simmering. Then remove from heat, cover and allow to cool. When cool, reheat until simmering and strain into warmed tankards, glasses or cups and enjoy it while hot. A slice of lemon placed on the surface of each drink adds an appetizing touch.

Lambs wool

An ancient recipe which offers a wholesome snack as well as an invigorating drink.

Ingredients: To make 1 pint (½ litre)

Ale or beer – 1 pint (½ litre)

Cooking apples – 2 large ones

Pure honey – 2 level tablespoons

Ground nutmeg – 2 level teaspoons

Method

Wash and dry the cooking apples. Cut out and discard the cores. This is most easily done by cutting around and through the centre of the apples with a coring knife. However, any small knife will do, providing you take care not to cut yourself. Place the cored apples on an oven proof tray and fill each hole with 1 level tablespoon of pure honey. Sprinkle 1 level teaspoon of ground nutmeg over each apple and then bake in a preheated moderate oven, gas no. 4 (350° F) for about 30 minutes. Then remove the oven proof tray and baked apples and pour the juice into a large saucepan. Put the apples on a plate or plates and set aside to cool. Add 1 pint (½ litre) of ale or beer to the juice in your saucepan; stir and heat until simmering. Then strain into warmed tankards, glasses or cups and drink while hot, taking a mouthful or spoonful of the delicious baked apple between sips.

17

CHEERS!

What's yours?

The following recipes offer a guide to help you brew quality ale, beer, lager and stout. Try them in 1 gallon (4½ litre) quantities to begin with and when you have completed the pleasurable task of sampling different brews you may like to make your favourites in larger batches.

Equipment and ingredients

All the items of equipment you need and ingredients specified in recipes are stocked by your local homebrew and/or health food stockist. The friendly, specialist staff are always pleased to help and advise you.

Special brews

Remember, the key to progressive home brewing is experiment. Once you have mastered the basics of brewing, begin to develop your own special brews. Keep a careful record of your recipes – the successful AND not quite so successful ones, and you will soon find yourself learning from experience. This is the only way to learn.

Caution

Please treat all the brews in this book with the respect their alcohol content demands.

CHEERS!

18

QUICK INDEX
TO BREWING PRINCIPLES AND METHODS

19

BEER AND ALE RECIPES

BEST BITTERS

Best Bitter Beer

  Delicious bitter brew. Lovely blend of ingredients. Medium strength. Enjoyable 6 weeks after being bottled or barrelled.

  Alcohol content about 4% alcohol by volume (7% proof).

Ingredients: To make 1 gallon (4½ litres)

Modern, economy recipe

Pure malt extract syrup – 8 oz (227 gms)
  or dried powder – 6 oz (170 gms)
Granulated sugar – 6 oz (170 gms)

Modern, sugar-free recipe
  Pure malt extract syrup – 1 lb (454 gms)
    or dried powder – 12 oz (340 gms)

Both recipes

Dried hops – 1½ oz (42 gms)
Cracked crystal malt grains – 2 oz (56 gms)
Epsom salts *(optional)* – ¼ (5 ml) teaspoon
Brewed tea, strong – 1 level tablespoon
Pure lemon juice – 1 level teaspoon (5 mls)
Beer yeast starter bottle
and
Water to 1 gallon (4½ litres)

Things to do before you begin brewing

a) *Beer yeast starter bottle*

  Activate the quantity of beer yeast recommended by the

manufácturer in a starter bottle (see page 33) at least an hour before preparing ingredients for brewing.

b) If you have not bought ready-cracked crystal malt grains, soak the uncracked grains for an hour in warm water and then crack them with a rolling pin.

c) Make a cup of fresh tea. Cover and allow to cool, or use cold tea from an earlier brew.

d) Extract required amount of juice from lemon and store in a covered, sterilised and rinsed cup until needed.

Method

When your beer yeast starter bottle is active and beginning to froth, simmer about 5 pints (3 litres) of water in a large saucepan and stir in malt extract (and granulated sugar and Epsom salts, *if you are using them*). Keep stirring until dissolved. Then add cracked crystal malt grains and ½ total measure of dried hops. Cover and simmer gently for 15 minutes. Then add remaining ½ of dried hops. Cover and simmer for 10 minutes. Then switch off heat and allow to cool. *When cool*, strain your brew into a bucket or brewing bin and cover. Discard solids. Add the activated beer yeast from your starter bottle to the brew and strained cold tea and pure lemon juice. Add enough cold water to bring the total amount of liquid to the quantity of beer you require. Allow at least 2 inches (51 mm)–4 inches (102 mm) head space at the top of your bucket or bin for frothing and foaming. Cover and place somewhere warm to ferment, about 18°C (64°F) is ideal. Leave 6–10 days to finish fermenting and then bottle or barrel.

Your best bitter beer remains in excellent condition in bottles for up to 7 months, after which its quality starts to decline.

When stored in a plastic pressure barrel your best bitter beer should stay in good condition for about 4 months, although its quality may begin a slow decline once the first few pints have been drawn off.

Extra Special Bitter Beer

Beer for the connoisseur. Strong, nourishing, well hopped and full flavoured bitter. Ready to drink 8 weeks after being bottled or barrelled.

Alcohol content about 6% alcohol by volume (10.5% proof).

Ingredients: To make 1 gallon (4½ litres)
Modern, economy recipe
Pure malt extract syrup – 12 oz (340 gms)
  or dried powder – 9 oz (255 gms)
Granulated sugar – 11 oz (312 gms)

Modern, sugar-free recipe
Pure malt extract syrup – 1½ lbs (680 gms)
  or dried powder – 1¼ lbs (567 gms)

Both recipes
Dried hops – 1½ oz (42 gms)
Cracked crystal malt grains – 3 oz (85 gms)
Epsom salts *(optional)* – ¼ (5 ml) teaspoon
Brewed tea, strong – 1 level tablespoon
Pure lemon juice – 1 level teaspoon (5 mls)
Beer yeast starter bottle
and
Water to 1 gallon (4½ litres)
Things to do before you begin brewing
a) *Beer yeast starter bottle*
  Activate the quantity of beer yeast recommended by the manufacturer in a starter bottle (see page 33) at least an hour before preparing ingredients for brewing.
b) If you have not bought ready-cracked crystal malt grains, soak the uncracked grains for an hour in warm water and then crack them with a rolling pin.
c) Make a cup of fresh tea. Cover and allow to cool, or use cold tea from an earlier brew.
d) Extract required amount of juice from lemon and store in a covered, sterilised and rinsed cup until needed.
Method
  When your beer yeast starter bottle is active and beginning to froth, simmer about 5 pints (3 litres) of water in a large saucepan and stir in malt extract (and granulated sugar and Epsom salts, *if you are using them*). Keep stirring until dissolved. Then add cracked crystal malt grains and ½ total measure of dried hops. Cover and simmer gently for 15 minutes. Then add remaining ½ of dried hops. Cover and simmer for 10 minutes. Then switch off heat

and allow to cool. *When cool*, strain your brew into a bucket or brewing bin and cover. Discard solids. Add the activated beer yeast from your starter bottle to the brew and strained cold tea and pure lemon juice. Add enough cold water to bring the total amount of liquid to the quantity of beer you require. Allow at least 2 inches (51 mm)–4 inches (102 mm) head space at the top of your bucket or bin for frothing and foaming. Cover and place somewhere warm to ferment, about 18°C (64°F) is ideal. Leave for 7–12 days to finish fermenting and then bottle or barrel.

Your extra special bitter beer remains in excellent condition in bottles for up to 9 months, after which its quality starts to decline.

When stored in a plastic pressure barrel your extra special bitter beer should stay in good condition for about 6 months, although its quality may begin a slow decline once the first few pints have been drawn off.

TRADITIONAL COUNTRY ALES
Apple Ale
Fruity light ale. Invigorating, refreshing and exciting drink. Sparkles with life and vitality. Once commonly enjoyed by country folk.

*Any pure fruit juice, bought from your local health food stockist, may be used in place of pure apple juice to produce an authentic traditional country-style fruit ale.

Ready to sample 6 weeks after the ale has been bottled or barrelled.

Alcohol content about 4% alcohol by volume (7% proof).

*Use only pure juice bought from your health food stockist.

Ingredients: To make 1 gallon (4½ litres)
Country recipe
Pure malt extract syrup – 8 oz (227 gms)
  or dried powder – 6 oz (170 gms)
Granulated sugar – 6 oz (170 gms)

Natural, sugar-free recipe
Pure malt extract syrup – 1 lb (454 gms)
  or dried powder – 12 oz (340 gms)

Both recipes
Pure apple juice – 1 pint (½ litre)
Cracked crystal malt grains – 1 oz (28 gms)
Brewed tea, strong – 1 level tablespoon
Pure lemon juice – 1 level teaspoon (5 mls)
Beer yeast starter bottle
and
Water to 1 gallon (4½ litres)
Things to do before you begin brewing
a) *Beer yeast starter bottle*

Activate the quantity of beer yeast recommended by the manufacturer in a starter bottle (see page 33) at least an hour before preparing ingredients for brewing.
b) If you have not bought ready-cracked crystal malt grains, soak the uncracked grains for an hour in warm water and then crack them with a rolling pin.
c) Make a cup of fresh tea. Cover and allow to cool, or use cold tea from an earlier brew.
d) Extract required amount of juice from lemon and store in a covered, sterilised and rinsed cup until needed.
Method

When your beer yeast starter bottle is active and beginning to froth, simmer about 5 pints (3 litres) of water in a large saucepan and stir in malt extract (and granulated sugar, *if you are using it*). Keep stirring until dissolved. Then add cracked crystal malt grains. Cover and simmer gently for 25 minutes. Then switch off heat. Cover and allow to cool. *When cool*, strain your brew into a bucket or brewing bin; add apple juice and cover. Discard solids. Add the activated beer yeast from your starter bottle to the brew and strained cold tea and pure lemon juice. Add enough cold water to bring the total amount of liquid to the quantity of ale you require. Allow at least 2 inches (51 mm)–4 inches (102 mm) head space at the top of your bucket or bin for frothing and foaming. Cover and place somewhere warm to ferment, about 18°C (64°F) is ideal. Leave for 6–10 days to finish fermenting and then bottle or barrel.

Your apple ale remains in excellent condition in bottles for up to 7 months, after which its quality starts to decline.

When stored in a plastic pressure barrel your apple ale should stay in good condition for about 4 months, although its quality may begin a slow decline once the first few pints have been drawn off.

Elizabethan Herb Ale

Flavourful and enjoyable ale. Full of goodness. Ready for drinking 8 weeks after being bottled or barrelled.

Alcohol content about 6% alcohol by volume (10.5% proof).

You may replace the herbs recommended in this recipe with a similar measure of herbs of your choice. They will impart their flavour and medicinal and health-giving properties to the ale. Favourite country herb ales include agrimony, borage, mint, parsley and thyme.

Tudor and Elizabethan ales were often highly spiced and reflect the excitement, zest for life, experiment and spirit of discovery characteristic of the age.

You can replace the herbs in the specimen recipe below with an equal quantity of spices. Popular spiced ales include balm, carraway seeds, cloves, marjoram and nutmeg.

Ingredients: To make 1 gallon (4½ litres)
Country, sugar-free recipe
Pure malt extract syrup – 1 lb (454 gms)
  or dried powder – 12 oz (340 gms)
Fresh bay leaves – 2 oz (56 gms)
  or dried – ½ oz (14 gms)
Fresh comfrey leaves – 2 oz (56 gms)
  or dried – ½ level (5 ml) teaspoon
Fresh rosemary leaves – 2 oz (56 gms)
  or dried – ½ level (5 ml) teaspoon
Pure honey – 8 oz (227 gms)
Cracked crystal malt grains – 1 oz (28 gms)
Brewed tea, strong – 1 level tablespoon
Pure lemon juice – 1 level teaspoon (5 mls)
Beer yeast starter bottle
and
Water to 1 gallon (4½ litres)
Things to do before you begin brewing
a) *Beer yeast starter bottle*

Activate the quantity of beer yeast recommended by the manufacturer in a starter bottle (see page 33) at least an hour before preparing ingredients for brewing.

b) If you have not bought ready-cracked crystal malt grains, soak the uncracked grains for an hour in warm water and then crack them with a rolling pin.

c) Make a cup of fresh tea. Cover and allow to cool, or use cold tea from an earlier brew.

d) Extract required amount of juice from lemon and store in a covered, sterilised and rinsed cup until needed.

e) If you are using fresh herbs, rinse the leaves in cold water.

Method

When your beer yeast starter bottle is active and beginning to froth, simmer about 5 pints (3 litres) of water in a large saucepan and stir in malt extract. Keep stirring until dissolved. Then add cracked crystal malt grains and ½ total measure of each herb. Cover and simmer gently for 15 minutes. Then add remaining ½ of herbs and all the pure honey; stir until dissolved. Cover and simmer for 10 minutes. Then switch off heat and allow to cool. *When cool*, strain your brew into a bucket or brewing bin and cover. Discard solids. Add the activated beer yeast from your starter bottle to the brew and strained cold tea and pure lemon juice. Add enough cold water to bring the total amount of liquid to the quantity of ale you require. Allow at least 2 inches (51 mm)–4 inches (102 mm) head space at the top of your bucket or bin for frothing and foaming. Cover and place somewhere warm to ferment, about 18°C (64°F) is ideal. Leave for 7–12 days to finish fermenting and then bottle or barrel.

Your herb ale remains in excellent condition in bottles for up to 9 months, after which its quality starts to decline.

When stored in a plastic pressure barrel your herb ale should stay in good condition for about 6 months, although its quality may begin a slow decline once the first few pints have been drawn off.

Ginger Ale

Strong, warming and full bodied ale. Marvellous tonic when feeling jaded. Drinkable 8 weeks after being bottled or barrelled.

Alcohol content about 6% alcohol by volume (10.5% proof). This is nothing like commercial "ginger ale" which is non-alcoholic.

Ingredients: To make 1 gallon (4½ litres)
Country recipe
Pure malt extract syrup – 8 oz (227 gms)
  or dried powder – 6 oz (170 gms)
Granulated sugar – 6 oz (170 gms)

Natural, sugar-free recipe
Pure malt extract syrup – 1 lb (454 gms)
  or dried powder – 12 oz (340 gms)

Both recipes
Pure honey – 8 oz (227 gms)
Root ginger – 2 oz (56 gms)
Cracked crystal malt grains – 1 oz (28 gms)
Brewed tea, strong – 1 level tablespoon
Pure lemon juice – 3 level teaspoons (15 mls)
Beer yeast starter bottle
and
Water to 1 gallon (4½ litres)
Things to do before you begin brewing
a) *Beer yeast starter bottle*
   Activate the quantity of beer yeast recommended by the manufacturer in a starter bottle (see page 33) at least an hour before preparing ingredients for brewing.
b) If you have not bought ready-cracked crystal malt grains, soak the uncracked grains for an hour in warm water and then crack them with a rolling pin.
c) Make a cup of fresh tea. Cover and allow to cool, or use cold tea from an earlier brew.
d) Extract required amount of juice from lemon and store in a covered, sterilised and rinsed cup until needed.
e) Bruise root ginger by crushing it with a rolling pin or hammer.
Method
   When your beer yeast starter bottle is active and beginning to froth, simmer about 5 pints (3 litres) of water in a large saucepan and stir in malt extract (and granulated sugar, *if you are using it*). Keep stirring until dissolved. Then add cracked crystal malt grains and all the bruised ginger. Cover and simmer gently for 15 minutes. Then add the pure honey; stir until dissolved. Cover and simmer for

10 minutes. Then switch off heat and allow to cool. *When cool*, strain your brew into a bucket or brewing bin and cover. Discard solids. Add the activated beer yeast from your starter bottle to the brew and strained cold tea and pure lemon juice. Add enough cold water to bring the total amount of liquid to the quantity of ale you require. Allow at least 2 inches (51 mm)–4 inches (102 mm) head space at the top of your bucket or bin for frothing and foaming. Cover and place somewhere warm to ferment, about 18°C (64°F) is ideal. Leave for 7–12 days to finish fermenting and then bottle or barrel.

Your ginger ale remains in excellent condition in bottles for up to 9 months, after which its quality starts to decline.

When stored in a plastic pressure barrel your ginger ale should stay in good condition for about 6 months, although its quality may begin a slow decline once the first few pints have been drawn off.

Nettle Ale

Popular English country ale. Biting, dry tang. A drink with a sting in its tail. Packed with vitamins. Enjoyable 8 weeks after being bottled or barrelled.

Alcohol content about 5% alcohol by volume (9% proof).

*Gather young nettle tops for best results.

Ingredients: To make 1 gallon (4½ litres)
Country recipe
Pure malt extract syrup – 8 oz (227 gms)
  or dried powder – 6 oz (170 gms)
Granulated sugar – 6 oz (170 gms)

Natural, sugar-free recipe
Pure malt extract syrup – 1 lb (454 gms)
  or dried powder – 12 oz (340 gms)

Both recipes
Nettle tops – 2 pints (1¼ litres)
Pure honey – 5 oz (142 gms)
Cracked crystal malt grains – 1 oz (28 gms)
Brewed tea, strong – 1 level tablespoon
Pure lemon juice – 3 level teaspoons (15 mls)

Beer yeast starter bottle
and
Water to 1 gallon (4½ litres)
Things to do before you begin brewing
a) *Beer yeast starter bottle*

Activate the quantity of beer yeast recommended by the manufacturer in a starter bottle (see page 33) at least an hour before preparing ingredients for brewing.

b) If you have not bought ready-cracked crystal malt grains, soak the uncracked grains for an hour in warm water and then crack them with a rolling pin.

c) Make a cup of fresh tea. Cover and allow to cool, or use cold tea from an earlier brew.

d) Extract required amount of juice from lemon and store in a covered, sterilised and rinsed cup until needed.

e) To measure young nettle tops, cut off and discard stalks and gently press tops in measuring jug. Then rinse them in cold water.

Method

When your beer yeast starter bottle is active and beginning to froth, simmer about 5 pints (3 litres) of water in a large saucepan and stir in malt extract (and granulated sugar *if you are using it*). Keep stirring until dissolved. Then add cracked crystal malt grains and ½ total measure of nettle tops. Cover and simmer gently for 15 minutes. Then add remaining ½ of nettle tops and all the pure honey; stir until dissolved. Cover and simmer for 10 minutes. Then switch off heat and allow to cool. *When cool*, strain your brew into a bucket or brewing bin, and cover. Discard solids. Add the activated beer yeast from your starter bottle to the brew and strained cold tea and pure lemon juice. Add enough cold water to bring the total amount of liquid to the quantity of ale you require. Allow at least 2 inches (51 mm)–4 inches (102 mm) head space at the top of your bucket or bin for frothing and foaming. Cover and place somewhere warm to ferment, about 18°C (64°F) is ideal. Leave for 7–12 days to finish fermenting and then bottle or barrel.

Your nettle ale remains in excellent condition in bottles for up to 9 months, after which its quality starts to decline.

When stored in a plastic pressure barrel your nettle ale should stay in good condition for about 6 months, although its quality may begin a slow decline once the first few pints have been drawn off.

Sack

Shakespeare's Sir Toby Belch thrived on a beverage similar to this one. Excellent drink. Full of flavour and nourishment. It helped put the merriment into Merrie England. Ready to enjoy 8 weeks after being bottled or barrelled.

Alcohol content about 6% alcohol by volume (10.5% proof).

Ingredients: To make 1 gallon (4½ litres)

Country, sugar-free recipe

Pure malt extract syrup – 1 lb (454 gms)
  or dried powder – 12 oz (340 gms)
Dried fennel seeds – 1 oz (28 gms)
Fresh rue sprays – 4
  or dried rue – ½ oz (14 gms)
Pure honey – 8 oz (227 gms)
Cracked crystal malt grains – 1 oz (28 gms)
Brewed tea, strong – 1 level tablespoon
Pure lemon juice – 1 level teaspoon (5 mls)
Beer yeast starter bottle
and
Water to 1 gallon (4½ litres)

Things to do before you begin brewing

a) *Beer yeast starter bottle*

Activate the quantity of beer yeast recommended by the manufacturer in a starter bottle (see page 33) at least an hour before preparing ingredients for brewing.

b) If you have not bought ready-cracked crystal malt grains, soak the uncracked grains for an hour in warm water and then crack them with a rolling pin.

c) Make a cup of fresh tea. Cover and allow to cool, or use cold tea from an earlier brew.

d) Extract required amount of juice from lemon and store in a covered, sterilised and rinsed cup until needed.

e) Rinse fresh rue sprays in cold water.

Method

When your beer yeast starter bottle is active and beginning to froth, simmer about 5 pints (3 litres) of water in a large saucepan and stir in malt extract. Keep stirring until dissolved. Then add cracked crystal malt grains and ½ total measure of rue and fennel seeds. Cover and simmer gently for 15 minutes. Then add remaining ½ of rue and fennel seeds and all the pure honey; stir until dissolved. Cover and simmer for 10 minutes. Then switch off heat and allow to cool. *When cool*, strain your brew into a bucket or brewing bin and cover. Discard solids. Add the activated beer yeast from your starter bottle to the brew and strained cold tea and pure lemon juice. Add enough cold water to bring the total amount of liquid to the quantity of sack you require. Allow at least 2 inches (51 mm)–4 inches (102 mm) head space at the top of your bucket or bin for frothing and foaming. Cover and place somewhere warm to ferment, about 18°C (64°F) is ideal. Leave for 7–12 days to finish fermenting and then bottle or barrel.

Your sack remains in excellent condition in bottles for up to 9 months, after which its quality starts to decline.

When stored in a plastic pressure barrel your sack should stay in good condition for about 6 months, although its quality may begin a slow decline once the first few pints have been drawn off.

Saxon Honey Ale
This style of ale was enjoyed in Saxon England. Drink some and know why King Alfred forgot those cakes. A rich, powerful ale. Drinkable 8 weeks after being bottled or barrelled.

Alcohol content about 7% alcohol by volume (12% proof).
Ingredients: To make 1 gallon (4½ litres)
Country, sugar-free recipe
Pure malt extract syrup – 8 oz (227 gms)
  or dried powder – 6 oz (170 gms)
Pure honey – 1 lb (454 gms)
Cracked crystal malt grains – 1 oz (28 gms)
Brewed tea, strong – 1 level tablespoon
Pure lemon juice – 3 level teaspoons (15 mls)
Beer yeast starter bottle
and
Water to 1 gallon (4½ litres)
Things to do before you begin brewing
a) *Beer yeast starter bottle*
Activate the quantity of beer yeast recommended by the manufacturer in a starter bottle (see page 33) at least an hour before preparing ingredients for brewing.

b) If you have not bought ready-cracked crystal malt grains, soak the uncracked grains for an hour in warm water and then crack them with a rolling pin.

c) Make a cup of fresh tea. Cover and allow to cool, or use cold tea from an earlier brew.

d) Extract required amount of juice from lemon and store in a covered, sterilised and rinsed cup until needed.

Method

When your beer yeast starter bottle is active and beginning to froth, simmer about 5 pints (3 litres) of water in a large saucepan and stir in malt extract. Keep stirring until dissolved. Then add cracked crystal malt grains. Cover and simmer gently for 15 minutes. Then add all the pure honey; stir until dissolved. Cover and simmer for 10 minutes. Then switch off heat and allow to cool.

When cool, strain your brew into a bucket or brewing bin and cover. Discard solids. Add the activated beer yeast from your starter bottle to the brew and strained cold tea and pure lemon juice. Add enough cold water to bring the total amount of liquid to the quantity of ale you require. Allow at least 2 inches (51 mm)–4 inches (102 mm) head space at the top of your bucket or bin for frothing and foaming. Cover and place somewhere warm to ferment, about 18°C (64°F) is ideal. Leave for 7–12 days to finish fermenting and then bottle or barrel.

Your honey ale remains in excellent condition in bottles for up to 12 months, after which its quality starts to decline.

When stored in a plastic pressure barrel your honey ale should stay in good condition for about 7 months, although its quality may begin a slow decline once the first few pints have been drawn off.

Woodruff Ale

Delicious ale. An old English favourite, but you won't find it on draught in the saloon bar of the Dog and Duck. Ready to drink 6 weeks after being bottled or barrelled.

Alcohol content about 4% alcohol by volume (7% proof).

*You can replace the woodruff leaves in this recipe with a similar measure of any of the traditional English flower and herb ale flavourings like: dandelion *heads*, coltsfoot *heads*, elderflower *florets*, and sweet gale *leaves*.

Ingredients: To make 1 gallon (4½ litres)
Country recipe
Pure malt extract syrup – 8 oz (227 gms)
  or dried powder – 6 oz (170 gms)
Granulated sugar – 6 oz (170 gms)

Natural, sugar-free recipe
Pure malt extract syrup – 1 lb (454 gms)
  or dried powder – 12 oz (340 gms)

Both recipes
Fresh woodruff leaves – 4 oz (113 gms)
  or dried leaves – 1 oz (28 gms)
Cracked crystal malt grains – 1 oz (28 gms)
Brewed tea, strong – 1 level tablespoon
Pure lemon juice – 1 level teaspoon (5 mls)
Beer yeast starter bottle
and
Water to 1 gallon (4½ litres)
Things to do before you begin brewing
a) *Beer yeast starter bottle*

Activate the quantity of beer yeast recommended by the
manufacturer in a starter bottle (see page 33) at least an hour before
preparing ingredients for brewing.

b) If you have not bought ready-cracked crystal malt grains, soak
the uncracked grains for an hour in warm water and then crack
them with a rolling pin.

c) Make a cup of fresh tea. Cover and allow to cool, or use cold tea
from an earlier brew.

d) Extract required amount of juice from lemon and store in a
covered, sterilised and rinsed cup until needed.

e) If you are using fresh woodruff leaves, rinse them in cold water.
Method

When your beer yeast starter bottle is active and beginning to
froth, simmer about 5 pints (3 litres) of water in a large saucepan

and stir in malt extract (and granulated sugar *if you are using it*). Keep stirring until dissolved. Then add cracked crystal malt grains and ½ total measure of woodruff leaves. Cover and simmer gently for 15 minutes. Then add remaining ½ of woodruff leaves. Cover and simmer for 10 minutes. Then switch off heat and allow to cool. *When cool*, strain your brew into a bucket or brewing bin and cover. Discard solids. Add the activated beer yeast from your starter bottle to the brew and strained cold tea and pure lemon juice. Add enough cold water to bring the total amount of liquid to the quantity of ale you require. Allow at least 2 inches (51 mm) – 4 inches (102 mm) head space at the top of your bucket or bin for frothing and foaming. Cover and place somewhere warm to ferment, about 18°C (64°F) is ideal. Leave for 6–10 days to finish fermenting and then bottle or barrel.

Your woodruff ale remains in excellent condition in bottles for up to 7 months, after which its quality starts to decline.

When stored in a plastic pressure barrel your woodruff ale should stay in good condition for about 4 months, although its quality may begin a slow decline once the first few pints have been drawn off.

VICTORIAN ALES
Victorian Old Ale

Strong, rich, golden ale. Old ale or India Pale Ale (I.P.A.) was originally brewed for British troops serving in India. There were riots when its alcohol content was reduced from about 10.5%

alcohol by volume (18.5% proof) to 6.5% alcohol by volume (11% proof). Imagine what those troops would think of our average commercial ale, at about 3.5% alcohol by volume (6% proof)!

This recipe brews an ale ready for drinking 8 weeks after being bottled or barrelled.

Alcohol content about 6% alcohol by volume (10.5% proof).

No riots, please.

Ingredients: To make 1 gallon (4½ litres)

Victorian, sugar-free recipe

Pure malt extract syrup – 1 lb (454 gms)
   or dried powder – 12 oz (340 gms)

Dried hops – 1 oz (28 gms)

Pure honey – 8 oz (227 gms)

Cracked crystal malt grains – 1 oz (28 gms)

Flaked barley – 1 oz (28 gms)

Black malt grains – 1 oz (28 gms)

Bran – 2 oz (56 gms)

Brewed tea, strong – 1 level tablespoon

Pure lemon juice – 1 level teaspoon (5 mls)

Beer yeast starter bottle

and

Water to 1 gallon (4½ litres)

Things to do before you begin brewing

a) *Beer yeast starter bottle*

Activate the quantity of beer yeast recommended by the manufacturer in a starter bottle (see page 33) at least an hour before preparing ingredients for brewing.

b) If you have not bought ready-cracked crystal malt grains, soak the uncracked grains for an hour in warm water and then crack them with a rolling pin.

c) DO NOT crack the black malt grains, use them as they are. If cracked, their flavour in your brew will be too strong. The flaked barley may be used as it is.

d) Make a cup of fresh tea. Cover and allow to cool, or use cold tea from an earlier brew.

e) Extract required amount of juice from lemon and store in a covered, sterilised and rinsed cup until needed.

Method

When your beer yeast starter bottle is active and beginning to froth, simmer about 6 pints (3½ litres) of water in a large saucepan and stir in malt extract. Keep stirring until dissolved. Then add cracked crystal malt grains, flaked barley, black malt grains and bran and ½ total measure of dried hops. Cover and simmer gently for 15 minutes. Then add remaining ½ of dried hops and all the pure honey; stir until dissolved. Cover and simmer for 10 minutes. Then switch off heat and allow to cool. *When cool*, strain your brew into a bucket or brewing bin and cover. Discard solids. Add the activated beer yeast from your starter bottle to the brew and strained cold tea and pure lemon juice. Add enough cold water to bring the total amount of liquid to the quantity of ale you require. Allow at least 2 inches (51 mm)–4 inches (102 mm) head space at the top of your bucket or bin for frothing and foaming. Cover and place somewhere warm to ferment, about 18°C (64°F) is ideal. Leave for 7–12 days to finish fermenting and then bottle or barrel.

Your Victorian old ale remains in excellent condition in bottles for up to 9 months, after which its quality starts to decline.

When stored in a plastic pressure barrel your Victorian old ale should stay in good condition for about 6 months, although its quality may begin a slow decline once the first few pints have been drawn off.

Porter

Originally, a mixture of ale and beer, coloured by roasted cereal grains and favoured by market porters in London. A working-class breakfast beverage in Victorian England – fortified the drinker in preparation for the long, hard day's labour ahead.

Strong, full bodied ale. Enjoyable 8 weeks after being bottled or barrelled.

Alcohol content about 6% alcohol by volume (10.5% proof).

Ingredients: To make 1 gallon (4½ litres)

Victorian, economy recipe

Pure malt extract syrup – 12 oz (340 gms)
  or dried powder – 9 oz (255 gms)
Granulated sugar – 11 oz (312 gms)

Victorian, sugar-free recipe
Pure malt extract syrup – 1½ lbs (680 gms)
  or dried powder – 1¼ lbs (567 gms)

Both recipes
Dried hops – 1 oz (28 gms)
Flaked barley – 1 oz (28 gms)
Black malt grains – 2 oz (56 gms)
Brewed tea, strong – 1 level tablespoon
Pure lemon juice – 1 level teaspoon (5 mls)
Beer yeast starter bottle
and
Water to 1 gallon (4½ litres)

Things to do before you begin brewing

a) *Beer yeast starter bottle*

Activate the quantity of beer yeast recommended by the manufacturer in a starter bottle (see page 33) at least an hour before preparing ingredients for brewing.

b) DO NOT crack the black malt grains, use them as they are. If cracked, their flavour in your brew will be too strong. The flaked barley may be used as it is.

c) Make a cup of fresh tea. Cover and allow to cool, or use cold tea from an earlier brew.

d) Extract required amount of juice from lemon and store in a covered, sterilised and rinsed cup until needed.

Method

When your beer yeast starter bottle is active and beginning to froth, simmer about 5 pints (3 litres) of water in a large saucepan and stir in malt extract (and granulated sugar, *if you are using it*). Keep stirring until dissolved. Then add flaked barley, black malt grains and ½ total measure of dried hops. Cover and simmer gently for 15 minutes. Then add remaining ½ of dried hops. Cover and simmer for 10 minutes. Then switch off heat and allow to cool. *When cool*, strain your brew into a bucket or brewing bin and cover. Discard solids. Add the activated beer yeast from your starter bottle to the brew and strained cold tea and pure lemon juice. Add enough cold water to bring the total amount of liquid to the quantity of ale you require. Allow at least 2 inches (51 mm)–4 inches (102 mm) head space at the top of your bucket or bin for frothing and foaming. Cover and place somewhere warm to ferment, about 18°C (64°F) is ideal. Leave for 7–12 days to finish fermenting and then bottle or barrel.

Your porter remains in excellent condition in bottles for up to 9 months, after which its quality starts to decline.

When stored in a plastic pressure barrel your porter should stay in good condition for about 6 months, although its quality may begin a slow decline once the first few pints have been drawn off.

MODERN ALES
Forest Brown Ale

Glorious brown ale. Appetising flavour and inviting colour. Enjoyable 6 weeks after being bottled or barrelled.

Alcohol content about 4% alcohol by volume (7% proof).
Ingredients: To make 1 gallon (4½ litres)
Modern, economy recipe
Pure malt extract syrup – 8 oz (227 gms)
 or dried powder – 6 oz (170 gms)
Granulated sugar – 6 oz (170 gms)

Modern, sugar-free recipe
Pure malt extract syrup – 1 lb (454 gms)
 or dried powder – 12 oz (340 gms)

Both recipes
Dried hops – 1 oz (28 gms)
Cracked crystal malt grains – 1 oz (28 gms)

Black malt grains – 2½ oz (71 gms)
Salt *(optional)* – ½ (5 ml) teaspoon
Brewed tea, strong – 1 level tablespoon
Pure lemon juice – 1 level teaspoon (5 mls)
Beer yeast starter bottle
and
Water to 1 gallon (4½ litres)
Things to do before you begin brewing
a) *Beer yeast starter bottle*
 Activate the quantity of beer yeast recommended by the manufacturer in a starter bottle (see page 33) at least an hour before preparing ingredients for brewing.
b) If you have not bought ready-cracked crystal malt grains, soak the uncracked grains for an hour in warm water and then crack them with a rolling pin.
c) DO NOT crack the black malt grains, use them as they are. If cracked, their flavour in your brew will be too strong.
d) Make a cup of fresh tea. Cover and allow to cool, or use cold tea from an earlier brew.
e) Extract required amount of juice from lemon and store in a covered, sterilised and rinsed cup until needed.
Method
 When your beer yeast starter bottle is active and beginning to froth, simmer about 5 pints (3 litres) of water in a large saucepan and stir in malt extract (and granulated sugar and salt, *if you are using them*). Keep stirring until dissolved. Then add cracked crystal malt grains, black malt grains and ½ total measure of dried hops. Cover and simmer gently for 15 minutes. Then add remaining ½ of dried hops. Cover and simmer for 10 minutes. Then switch off heat and allow to cool. *When cool*, strain your brew into a bucket or brewing bin and cover. Discard solids. Add the activated beer yeast from your starter bottle to the brew and strained cold tea and pure lemon juice. Add enough cold water to bring the total amount of liquid to the quantity of ale you require. Allow at least 2 inches (51 mm)–4 inches (102 mm) head space at the top of your bucket or bin for frothing and foaming. Cover and place somewhere warm to ferment, about 18°C (64°F) is ideal. Leave for 6–10 days to finish fermenting and then bottle or barrel.
 Your Forest brown ale remains in excellent condition in bottles

for up to 7 months, after which its quality starts to decline.

When stored in a plastic pressure barrel your Forest brown ale should stay in good condition for about 4 months, although its quality may begin a slow decline once the first few pints have been drawn off.

John's College Old Ale

Excellent, tasty ale. Beautifully smooth and refreshing drink. Ready to drink 6 weeks after being bottled or barrelled.

Alcohol content about 4% alcohol by volume (7% proof).
Ingredients: To make 1 gallon (4½ litres)
Modern, economy recipe
Pure malt extract syrup – 8 oz (227 gms)
   or dried powder – 6 oz (170 gms)
Granulated sugar – 6 oz (170 gms)

Modern, sugar-free recipe
Pure malt extract syrup – 1 lb (454 gms)
   or dried powder – 12 oz (340 gms)

Both recipes
Dried hops – 1 oz (28 gms)
Flaked maize – 1 oz (28 gms)
Flaked barley – 2 oz (56 gms)
Epsom salts *(optional)* – ¼ (5 ml) teaspoon
Brewed tea, strong – 1 level tablespoon
Pure lemon juice – 1 level teaspoon (5 mls)
Beer yeast starter bottle
and
Water to 1 gallon (4½ litres)
Things to do before you begin brewing
a) *Beer yeast starter bottle*

Activate the quantity of beer yeast recommended by the manufacturer in a starter bottle (see page 33) at least an hour before preparing ingredients for brewing.
b) Make a cup of fresh tea. Cover and allow to cool, or use cold tea from an earlier brew.
c) Extract required amount of juice from lemon and store in a

covered, sterilised and rinsed cup until needed.

Method

When your beer yeast starter bottle is active and beginning to froth, simmer about 5 pints (3 litres) of water in a large saucepan and stir in malt extract (and granulated sugar and Epsom salts, *if you are using them*). Keep stirring until dissolved. Then add flaked maize, flaked barley and ½ total measure of dried hops. Cover and simmer gently for 15 minutes. Then add remaining ½ of dried hops. Cover and simmer for 10 minutes. Then switch off heat and allow to cool. *When cool*, strain your brew into a bucket or brewing bin and cover. Discard solids. Add the activated beer yeast from your starter bottle to the brew and strained cold tea and pure lemon juice. Add enough cold water to bring the total amount of liquid to the quantity of ale you require. Allow at least 2 inches (51 mm)–4 inches (102 mm) head space at the top of your bucket or bin for frothing and foaming. Cover and place somewhere warm to ferment, about 18°C (64°F) is ideal. Leave for 6–10 days to finish fermenting and then bottle or barrel.

Your John's College old ale remains in excellent condition in bottles for up to 7 months, after which its quality starts to decline.

When stored in a plastic pressure barrel your John's College old ale should stay in good condition for about 4 months, although its quality may begin a slow decline once the first few pints have been drawn off.

Shire Light Ale

Light, fresh, tangy ale. Nice long drink. Ready to enjoy 6 weeks after being bottled or barrelled.

Alcohol content about 4% alcohol by volume (7% proof).

Ingredients: To make 1 gallon (4½ litres)

Modern, economy recipe

Pure malt extract syrup – 8 oz (227 gms)
 or dried powder – 6 oz (170 gms)
Granulated sugar – 6 oz (170 gms)

Modern, sugar-free recipe
Pure malt extract syrup – 1 lb (454 gms)
 or dried powder – 12 oz (340 gms)

Both recipes
Dried hops – 1 oz (28 gms)
Cracked crystal malt grains – 1 oz (28 gms)
Flaked barley – 1 oz (28 gms)
Epsom salts *(optional)* – ¼ (5 ml) teaspoon
Brewed tea, strong – 1 level tablespoon
Pure lemon juice – 1 level teaspoon (5 mls)
Beer yeast starter bottle
and
Water to 1 gallon (4½ litres)

Things to do before you begin brewing

a) *Beer yeast starter bottle*

Activate the quantity of beer yeast recommended by the manufacturer in a starter bottle (see page 33) at least an hour before preparing ingredients for brewing.

b) If you have not bought ready-cracked crystal malt grains, soak the uncracked grains for an hour in warm water and then crack them with a rolling pin. The flaked barley may be used as it is.

c) Make a cup of fresh tea. Cover and allow to cool, or use cold tea from an earlier brew.

d) Extract required amount of juice from lemon and store in a covered, sterilised and rinsed cup until needed.

Method

When your beer yeast starter bottle is active and beginning to froth, simmer about 5 pints (3 litres) of water in a large saucepan and stir in malt extract (and granulated sugar and Epsom salts, *if you are using them*). Keep stirring until dissolved. Then add cracked crystal malt grains, flaked barley and ½ total measure of dried hops. Cover and simmer gently for 15 minutes. Then add remaining ½ of dried hops. Cover and simmer for 10 minutes. Then switch off heat and allow to cool. *When cool*, strain your brew into a bucket or brewing bin and cover. Discard solids. Add the activated beer yeast from your starter bottle to the brew and strained cold tea and pure lemon juice. Add enough cold water to bring the total amount of liquid to the quantity of ale you require. Allow at least 2 inches (51 mm)–4 inches (102 mm) head space at the top of your bucket or bin for frothing and foaming. Cover and place somewhere warm to ferment, about 18°C (64°F) is ideal. Leave for 6 – 10 days to finish fermenting and then bottle or barrel.

Your Shire light ale remains in excellent condition in bottles for up to 7 months, after which its quality starts to decline.

When stored in a plastic pressure barrel your Shire light ale should stay in good condition for about 4 months, although its quality may begin a slow decline once the first few pints have been drawn off.

MODERN LAGERS
Munich Lager
German style lager. Superb quality. Strong, full bodied, smooth and golden. Savour every silken mouthful as you sip it down. For best results use a "lager" or light malt extract syrup or dried powder, see page 23. Ready to drink 8 weeks after being bottled or barrelled.

Alcohol content about 6% alcohol by volume (10.5% proof).
Ingredients: To make 1 gallon (4½ litres)
Modern, economy recipe
Pure malt extract syrup – 12 oz (340 gms)
 or dried powder – 9 oz (255 gms)
Granulated sugar – 11 oz (312 gms)

Modern, sugar-free recipe
Pure malt extract syrup – 1½ lbs (680 gms)
 or dried powder – 1¼ lbs (567 gms)

Both recipes
Dried Hallertau hops – 1 oz (28 gms)
Cracked crystal malt grains – 1 oz (28 gms)
Flaked maize – 3 oz (85 gms)
Brewed tea, strong – 1 level tablespoon
Pure lemon juice – 1 level teaspoon (5 mls)
Lager yeast starter bottle
and
Water to 1 gallon (4½ litres)
Things to do before you begin brewing
a) *Lager yeast starter bottle*
Activate the quantity of lager yeast recommended by the manufacturer in a starter bottle (see page 33) at least an hour before

preparing ingredients for brewing.

b) If you have not bought ready-cracked crystal malt grains, soak the uncracked grains for an hour in warm water and then crack them with a rolling pin.

c) Make a cup of fresh tea. Cover and allow to cool, or use cold tea from an earlier brew.

d) Extract required amount of juice from lemon and store in a covered, sterilised and rinsed cup until needed.

Method

When your lager yeast starter bottle is active and beginning to froth, simmer about 5 pints (3 litres) of water in a large saucepan and stir in malt extract (and granulated sugar, *if you are using it*). Keep stirring until dissolved. Then add cracked crystal malt grains, flaked maize and ½ total measure of dried hops. Cover and simmer gently for 15 minutes. Then add remaining ½ of dried hops. Cover and simmer for 10 minutes. Then switch off heat and allow to cool. *When cool*, strain your brew into a bucket or brewing bin and cover. Discard solids. Add the activated lager yeast from your starter bottle to the brew and strained cold tea and pure lemon juice. Add enough cold water to bring the total amount of liquid to the quantity of lager you require. Allow at least 2 inches (51 mm)–4 inches (102 mm) head space at the top of your bucket or bin for frothing and foaming. Cover and place somewhere warm to ferment, about 18°C (64°F) is ideal. Leave for 7–12 days to finish fermenting and then bottle or barrel.

Your Munich lager remains in excellent condition in bottles for up to 9 months, after which its quality starts to decline.

When stored in a plastic pressure barrel your Munich lager should stay in good condition for about 6 months, although its quality may begin a slow decline once the first few pints have been drawn off.

Scandinavian Lager

Rich, powerful lager. For best results, use a "lager" or light malt extract syrup or dried powder, see page 23. Ready to enjoy 6 weeks after being bottled or barrelled.

Alcohol content about 4.5% alcohol by volume (8% proof).

Ingredients: To make 1 gallon (4½ litres)
Modern, economy recipe
Pure malt extract syrup – 8 oz (227 gms)
   or dried powder – 6 oz (170 gms)
Granulated sugar – 6 oz (170 gms)

Modern, sugar-free recipe
Pure malt extract syrup – 1 lb (454 gms)
   or dried powder – 12 oz (340 gms)

Both recipes
Dried Hallertau hops – 1 oz (28 gms)
Pure honey – 2 heaped tablespoons ·
Cracked crystal malt grains – 1 oz (28 gms)
Flaked maize – 1 oz (28 gms)
Brewed tea, strong – 1 level tablespoon
Pure lemon juice – 1 level teaspoon (5 mls)
Lager yeast starter bottle
and
Water to 1 gallon (4½ litres)
Things to do before you begin brewing
a) *Lager yeast starter bottle*
   Activate the quantity of lager yeast recommended by the manufacturer in a starter bottle (see page 33) at least an hour before preparing ingredients for brewing.
b) If you have not bought ready-cracked crystal malt grains, soak the uncracked grains for an hour in warm water and then crack them with a rolling pin.
c) Make a cup of fresh tea. Cover and allow to cool, or use cold tea from an earlier brew.
d) Extract required amount of juice from lemon and store in a covered, sterilised and rinsed cup until needed.
Method
   When your lager yeast starter bottle is active and beginning to froth, simmer about 5 pints (3 litres) of water in a large saucepan and stir in malt extract (and granulated sugar, *if you are using it*). Keep stirring until dissolved. Then add cracked crystal malt grains, flaked maize and ½ total measure of dried hops. Cover and simmer gently for 15 minutes. Then add remaining ½ of dried hops and all

the pure honey; stir until dissolved. Cover and simmer for 10 minutes. Then switch off heat and allow to cool. *When cool*, strain your brew into a bucket or brewing bin and cover. Discard solids. Add the activated lager yeast from your starter bottle to the brew and strained cold tea and pure lemon juice. Add enough cold water to bring the total amount of liquid to the quantity of lager you require. Allow at least 2 inches (51 mm)–4 inches (102 mm) head space at the top of your bucket or bin for frothing and foaming. Cover and place somewhere warm to ferment, about 18°C (64°F) is ideal. Leave for 6–10 days to finish fermenting and then bottle or barrel.

Your Scandinavian lager remains in excellent condition in bottles for up to 7 months, after which its quality starts to decline.

When stored in a plastic pressure barrel your Scandinavian lager should stay in good condition for about 4 months, although its quality may begin a slow decline once the first few pints have been drawn off.

OTHER ALES
Barley Wine
Strong, full bodied beverage. Lots of flavour. Ready to drink 8 weeks after being bottled or barrelled.

Alcohol content about 8.5% by volume (14.5% proof).
Ingredients: To make 1 gallon (4½ litres)
Barley wine, economy recipe
Pure malt extract syrup – 12 oz (340 gms)
    or dried powder – 9 oz (255 gms)
Granulated sugar – 11 oz (312 gms)

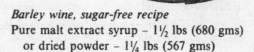

Barley wine, sugar-free recipe
Pure malt extract syrup – 1½ lbs (680 gms)
    or dried powder – 1¼ lbs (567 gms)

Both recipes
Dried hops – 1 oz (28 gms)
Pure honey – 8 oz (227 gms)
Cracked crystal malt grains – 4 oz (113 gms)
Black malt grains – 2½ oz (71 gms)
Flaked barley – 3 oz (85 gms)

Brewed tea, strong – 1 level tablespoon
Pure lemon juice – 3 level teaspoons (15 mls)
Beer yeast starter bottle
and
Water to 1 gallon (4½ litres)
Things to do before you begin brewing
a) *Beer yeast starter bottle*

Activate the quantity of beer yeast recommended by the manufacturer in a starter bottle (see page 33) at least an hour before preparing ingredients for brewing.

b) If you have not bought ready-cracked crystal malt grains, soak the uncracked grains for an hour in warm water and then crack them with a rolling pin.

c) DO NOT crack the black malt grains, use them as they are. If cracked, their flavour in your brew will be too strong. The flaked barley may be used as it is.

d) Make a cup of fresh tea. Cover and allow to cool, or use cold tea from an earlier brew.

e) Extract required amount of juice from lemon and store in a covered, sterilised and rinsed cup until needed.

Method

When your beer yeast starter bottle is active and beginning to froth, simmer about 6 pints (3½ litres) of water in a large saucepan and stir in malt extract (and granulated sugar, *if you are using it*). Keep stirring until dissolved. Then add cracked crystal malt grains, flaked barley, black malt grains and ½ total measure of dried hops. Cover and simmer gently for 15 minutes. Then add remaining ½ of dried hops and all the pure honey; stir until dissolved. Cover and simmer for 10 minutes. Then switch off heat and allow to cool. *When cool*, strain your brew into a bucket or brewing bin and cover. Discard solids. Add the activated beer yeast from your starter bottle to the brew and strained cold tea and pure lemon juice. Add enough cold water to bring the total amount of liquid to the quantity of barley wine you require. Allow at least 2 inches (51 mm) – 4 inches (102 mm) head space at the top of your bucket or bin for frothing and foaming. Cover and place somewhere warm to ferment, about 18°C (64°F) is ideal. Leave for 9–14 days to finish fermenting and then bottle or barrel.

Your barley wine remains in excellent condition in bottles for up to 12 months, after which its quality starts to decline.

When stored in a plastic pressure barrel your barley wine should stay in good condition for about 7 months, although its quality may begin a slow decline once the first few pints have been drawn off.

Stout

Vitalizing, wholesome brew. Feel it doing you good as it slips down. The first recipe for stout is commonly credited to eighteenth century Irishman, Arthur Guinness, who developed his brew while experimenting with roasted grains in beer. You see, there is the chance of an exciting discovery for us all. Ready to drink 8 weeks after being bottled or barrelled.

Alcohol content about 6% by volume (10.5% proof).

Ingredients: To make 1 gallon (4½ litres)

Stout, economy recipe

Pure malt extract syrup – 12 oz (340 gms)
  or dried powder – 9 oz (255 gms)
Granulated sugar – 11 oz (312 gms)

Stout, sugar-free recipe
Pure malt extract syrup – 1½ lbs (680 gms)
  or dried powder – 1¼ lbs (567 gms)

Both recipes

Dried hops – 1 oz (28 gms)
Cracked crystal malt grains – 3 oz (85 gms)
Black malt grains – 5 oz (142 gms)
Brown rice – 1 oz (28 gms)
Salt *(optional)* – ½ level (5 ml) teaspoon
Brewed tea, strong – 1 level tablespoon
Pure lemon juice – 2 level teaspoons (10 mls)
Beer yeast starter bottle
and
Water to 1 gallon (4½ litres)

Things to do before you begin brewing

a) *Beer yeast starter bottle*

Activate the quantity of beer yeast recommended by the manufacturer in a starter bottle (see page 33) at least an hour before preparing ingredients for brewing.

b) If you have not bought ready-cracked crystal malt grains, soak the uncracked grains for an hour in warm water and then crack them with a rolling pin.

c) DO NOT crack the black malt grains, use them as they are. If cracked, their flavour in your brew will be too strong. The brown rice may be used as it is.

d) Make a cup of fresh tea. Cover and allow to cool, or use cold tea from an earlier brew.

e) Extract required amount of juice from lemon and store in a covered, sterilised and rinsed cup until needed.

Method

When your beer yeast starter bottle is active and beginning to froth, simmer about 6 pints ($3\frac{1}{2}$ litres) of water in a large saucepan and stir in malt extract (and granulated sugar and salt, *if you are using them*). Keep stirring until dissolved. Then add cracked crystal malt grains, black malt grains, rice and $\frac{1}{2}$ total measure of dried hops. Cover and simmer gently for 15 minutes. Then add remaining $\frac{1}{2}$ of dried hops. Cover and simmer for 10 minutes. Then switch off heat and allow to cool. *When cool*, strain your brew into a bucket or brewing bin and cover. Discard solids. Add the activated beer yeast from your starter bottle to the brew and strained cold tea and pure lemon juice. Add enough cold water to bring the total amount of liquid to the quantity of stout you require. Allow at least 2 inches (51 mm)–4 inches (102 mm) head space at the top of your bucket or bin for frothing and foaming. Cover and place somewhere warm to ferment, about 18°C (64°F) is ideal. Leave for 7–12 days to finish fermenting and then bottle or barrel.

Your stout remains in excellent condition in bottles for up to 9 months, after which its quality starts to decline.

When stored in a plastic pressure barrel your stout should stay in good condition for about 6 months, although its quality may begin a slow decline once the first few pints have been drawn off.

20

CIDER, APPLES, LOVE
AND HEALTH

Ever since Eve gave Adam a bite of her fruit, the juicy, luscious apple has been linked with love, romance and vitality. The beautiful Greek goddess Juno gave Jupiter the golden apples of the Hesperides on their wedding day, and the wounded Celtic King Arthur was taken to the Vale of Avalon (Apple Vale) to be restored to full health. Numerous Greek, Roman, Scandinavian and Celtic legends refer to the magic power of apples in all matters concerning love and health.

These ancient stories do have a basis in fact, for the apple is full of nourishing goodness. Apples contain vitamins A, B, C and G (also known as B_2, riboflavin); protein, carbohydrates, calcium, iron, phosphorous and potassium.

A regular, moderate daily intake of apples, pure apple juice, or cider is said to prevent – or help cure: acne, anaemia, arthritis, asthma, catarrh, poor skin complexion and pyorrhea.

Apples, pure apple juice and cider are thought to stimulate all bodily functions, reduce emotional tension, headaches; aid digestion and prevent constipation.

21

CIDER: THE THINGS YOU NEED TO KNOW

Equipment

Equipment needed for making cider is much the same as equipment needed for brewing ale and beer. To save repeating all the information here, you may like to refer to Chapter 8, on page 28 in the brewing section of this book.

a) Food grade bucket or brewing bin, with lid.
b) Syphon tubing.
c) Polythene funnel.
d) Strainer.
e) Kitchen scales.
f) Measuring jug.
g) 1 pint (½ litre) home brew beer bottles.
h) Metal caps to fit home brew beer bottles.
i) Capping tool to fasten metal caps on home brew bottles.
j) A plastic pressure barrel, if you are making cider in large quantities and look forward to drinking it regularly.

k) A wire handled bottle brush for cleaning bottles and barrels.
In addition, you will require:

a) A kitchen mincer, either manual or electric.

b) A large wooden or plastic spoon for stirring.

c) One or more 1 gallon (4½ litre) narrow-necked glass or plastic vessels, in which first to ferment and then store the cider to mature before bottling or barrelling. These are sold by your local homebrew stockist.

d) Cotton wool, or air locks and *bored* cork or rubber bungs to plug into the tops of your 1 gallon (4½ litre) narrow-necked vessels while the cider is fermenting.

e) Cork or rubber bungs to seal the tops of your 1 gallon (4½ litre) narrow-necked vessels while the cider is maturing.

If you have access to lots of apples and wish to make your cider entirely from pure pressed apple juice, about 20 lbs (9 kgs) of apples is needed to make 1 gallon (4½ litres) of cider. This way, you will have to use a fruit press. You may know someone who has one, or you might like to buy a small purpose-made fruit press from your local homebrew stockist. If you are an accomplished D.I.Y. enthusiast you can make one using a car jack temporarily fitted into a stout wooden fame.

Super cider can be made using much smaller quantities of apples, combined with pure apple juice bought from your health food stockist and pure honey OR granulated sugar. Full details are given in recipes.

Cleanliness

Before use, sterilise ALL your equipment with sulphite solution (sodium metabisulphite mixed with water, see page 32) and then *rinse away* traces of the solution with warm water.

Ingredients

Commercial cider makers use a blend of cider apples to produce the final rich, smooth, golden bottled cider.

Their secret lies in extracting and mixing juice from sweet and bitter tasting apples. You will achieve best results by following their example and fermenting juice from a selection of apples chosen for their varying sweet and bitter flavours. A half sweet and half bitter mix gives superb results. However, you can make excellent cider using whichever types of apple are most readily available to you. Windfalls are ideal and pears may be used successfully in place of up to ½ the total measure of apples required for each recipe.

Perry

If you have access to large numbers of pears, you can make *perry*, a light cider-like drink, by substituting pears for the *entire* quantity of apples suggested in cider recipes in this book.

True perry is fermented from pure pressed pear juice. However, cider-perry is a gorgeous drink made from a combination of pears and apples.

Pure perry

To make pure perry, follow the Celtic cider recipe. You will need about 20 lbs (9 kgs) of pears to replace the whole quantity of apples and produce 1 gallon (4½ litres) of pure pear juice.

Cider-perry

Replace apples in each of the cider recipes except Celtic cider (see above) with an identical measure of pears. In addition use pure apple juice, bought from your health food stockist, as directed in recipes.

Prepare, ferment, mature, bottle or barrel and serve your perry in exactly the same way as cider.

22

MAKING CIDER

Fermenting cider

To ferment the natural sugar (fructose and glucose) content of pure apple juice and pure honey, and any granulated sugar (sucrose) you choose to add to your recipe in place of pure honey, use all-purpose wine yeast (saccharomyces ellipsoideus). During fermentation, wine yeast turns the natural sugar (fructose and glucose) and any granulated sugar (sucrose) into alcohol.

Forms of wine yeast

All-purpose wine yeast is available from your homebrew stockist and is marketed in dry granular form in tubs, sachets; as tablets in tubes and also as a pure, natural strain in a liquid or jelly medium in a phial.

Dried wine yeast compounds

Some dried wine yeast compounds contain tiny amounts of sugar (sucrose) and chemicals like ammonium chloride and ammonium phosphate dibasic. If you wish to make your cider completely free of sugar (sucrose) and chemicals, check the list of contents carefully before buying.

Wine yeast starter bottle

Wine yeast can be added directly to your cider ingredients, but, for an express start to fermentation, prepare a wine yeast starter bottle about 48 hours before you plan to start making your cider.

Method

a) Sterilise with sulphite solution (sodium metabisulphite mixed with water, see page 32) and *rinse* with warm water, a 1 pint (½ litre) bottle and polythene funnel.

b) Put the funnel in the mouth of your bottle and following the

manufacturer's instructions, measure sufficient wine yeast to
ferment 1 gallon (4½ litres) into the bottle.

c) Pour in ¾ pint (426 mls) of pure apple juice previously pressed
from apples or bought from your health food stockist. You can
count this ¾ pint (426 mls) of pure apple juice as part of the total
quantity of apple juice required to make your cider. Cover the
bottle with a 4 inch (102 mm) square of sterilised, rinsed polythene
smoothed over the bottle mouth and secured around the neck with
an elastic band, string or strong thread.

d) Keep the bottle in a warm place. The wine yeast multiplies in the
pure apple juice and within 48 hours should be active and ready to
start fermenting your cider.

Storage

After it has finished fermenting, all cider benefits from a period
of storage in 1 gallon (4½ litre) narrow-necked glass or plastic
vessels before being bottled or barrelled. During storage the cider
flavour develops and matures and the initially rough texture
rounds into a rich, velvet smoothness.

Recommended periods of storage for your cider, before bottling
or barrelling and serving, are given in recipes.

Clearing

Your cider should clear naturally, during storage. Tannin in the
tea and citric acid in the pure lemon juice added to recipes in this
book assist your cider's clearing. However, if the cider has not
cleared completely by the time you are ready to bottle or barrel it,
try this trick:

For each gallon (4½ litres) of cider you wish to clear:

a) Pour or syphon ½ cup of cloudy cider into a sterilised, rinsed
cup.

b) Add the white of 1 egg + 1 level tablespoon of strained, cold tea.

c) Mix ingredients thoroughly and pour back into the vessel of
cloudy cider.

d) Sterilise, rinse and refit the cork or rubber bung and store cider
in a cool place.

Your cider should clear within 3–5 weeks.

If you prefer, you can buy all sorts of commercial clearing
compounds from your local homebrew stockist.

Still or sparkling?
Sparkling cider

Sparkling cider is simply cider matured for the length of time suggested in the recipe, which has pure honey OR granulated sugar added to it before being bottled or barrelled. A secondary fermentation of the pure honey or granulated sugar takes place in the bottle or barrel, giving the cider natural life and sparkle and providing a protective covering of carbon dioxide gas, that keeps the sparkling cider in super condition longer than still cider. Refer to page 96 and recipes for details.

Still cider

Is mature, ready-for-bottling cider which is syphoned straight into bottles without the addition of pure honey or granulated sugar. Still cider does not sparkle and because there is no protective blanket of carbon dioxide gas it is unsuitable for barrelling and will not keep in bottles for as long as sparkling cider. See page 96 and recipes for full details.

Bottles

Some home cider makers bottle their sparkling cider in screw-top lemonade or commercial cider bottles. Such bottles are not designed to withstand the comparatively high pressure of carbon dioxide gas which can develop in your home made bottled cider and may explode!

For *safety's sake* use only specially manufactured 1 pint (½ litre) home brew beer bottles and bottle caps sold by your homebrew stockist, see page 30. Flying glass from burst bottles can cause serious physical injury – DO NOT TAKE RISKS.

This warning ALSO applies to your home made still cider. A chance secondary fermentation of any residual natural sugar (fructose and glucose) or granulated sugar (sucrose) in still cider stored in an unsuitable bottle could cause the bottle to *explode*.

Use home brew beer bottles for your sparkling AND still cider.

Plastic pressure barrels

May be used for storing and dispensing sparkling cider in the same way they are used for beer, see page 29.

Bottling or barrelling

Whether you have decided to bottle or barrel your cider, begin your bottling or barrelling this way:

1. *Sterilise and rinse:*
a) Syphon tubing
b) Plastic (food grade) bucket or brewing bin and lid.
c) Polythene funnel
2. Place your 1 gallon (4½ litre) narrow-necked vessel of clear, mature cider on a surface at a higher level than the bucket or brewing bin. Put one end of the syphon tubing in the cider so it rests just above the sediment. Suck some cider into the tube and place the open end in your bucket or brewing bin. Cider will flow from the vessel into your bucket or brewing bin. When only sediment remains in the vessel; cover the bucket or brewing bin and wash out, sterilise and rinse your 1 gallon (4½ litre) narrow-necked vessel. Store it away, ready for your next cider making session.

Bottling still cider

To bottle still cider scoop the cider from your bucket or brewing bin in a sterilised, rinsed jug, mug or cup and pour through the polythene funnel into sterilised, rinsed home brew beer bottles. Fill each bottle to within 1 inch (25 mm) of the top of the bottle. Then fasten a sterilised, rinsed metal cap with your capping tool, see page 40. When bottling *still cider only*, you may choose to use sterilised, rinsed reusable plastic caps.

Putting sparkle into cider

For each gallon (4½ litres) of cider you wish to make sparkle:
a) Take two or three cupfuls of cider from your bucket or brewing bin and pour into a sterilised, rinsed saucepan.
b) Heat the cider in your saucepan until simmering; then dissolve 2 level tablespoons of pure honey OR 1½ level tablespoons of granulated sugar. Cover and allow to cool.
WARNING – Never exceed the recommended measure of pure honey or granulated sugar, or your bottles may explode!
c) *When cool*, pour the sweetened cider from the saucepan into your bucket or brewing bin of cider. Stir vigorously. Cover and leave for about 10 minutes to blend and mix thoroughly.

Bottling sparkling cider

Fill your home brew beer bottles with sparkling cider in exactly the same way as you would still cider, see above. You should secure *metal caps only* on bottles of sparkling cider. To do this you will need a capping tool, see page 30. Re-usable plastic caps are often blown off by the force of carbon dioxide gas in sparkling cider and cannot be recommended.

Barrelling sparkling cider

Fill your plastic pressure barrel to its shoulder with sparkling cider, allowing 2–3 inches (51–76 mm) air space between its cap and the surface of your cider. Screw the cap on tightly.

Development in bottles or barrel

Your still and sparkling cider continues to develop and mature for several weeks after being bottled or barrelled. The recipes suggest when your cider should be ready to serve.

Serving cider

Cider tastes best if chilled in your fridge or a bowl of cold water, before being served.

Chilled sparkling or still cider complements salads, fish and white meat dishes and goes well with the traditional countryman's lunch of crusty wholemeal bread, cheese and pickles.

Sweetening cider

To sweeten one pint ($\frac{1}{2}$ litre) of cider, vigorously stir and dissolve one heaped tablespoon of pure honey OR one level tablespoon of caster sugar in the poured cider immediately before serving. Of course, you may vary the amount of pure honey or caster sugar to suit your taste, or the preference of guests.

23

CIDER VINEGAR FOR HEALTH AND FITNESS

Cider vinegar is becoming increasingly popular with health conscious people. It enhances nourishing, gourmet whole food meals AND is a marvellous aid to slim, trim healthiness.

For good health

There is considerable evidence to suggest that 2 level teaspoons (10 mls) of cider vinegar, mixed with 1 level teaspoon of pure honey in a glass of cold or warm water, taken three times a day after meals, will help slimmers to achieve their target weight and greatly benefit people suffering from arthritis, asthma, insomnia and rheumatism. It is also an excellent guard against the common cold.

For cooking

Many cordon bleu chefs use cider vinegar in preference to wine or malt vinegar. When you prepare a meal from organically raised, natural whole foods you will find the quality of most dishes improved by the addition of some cider vinegar. It also gives extra appeal to gravies, sauces, salad dressings and makes superb chutney and pickle.

Make your own

You may convert to vinegar any clear, mature cider which is ready for bottling. Simply follow these instructions:

a) Decide how much cider vinegar you wish to make and then dilute each pint (½ litre) of mature cider with ¼ pint (142 mls) of cold water and add ½ pint (284 mls) of commercial cider vinegar.

b) Half fill sterilised, rinsed bottles or a large narrow-necked vessel with the mixture and plug the top with cotton wool.

c) Keep it in a warm place for about eight weeks. During this time the cider vinegar will cloud and a skin form on its surface. When transformation to vinegar is complete the cider vinegar clears.

d) When clear and bright, syphon the cider vinegar off its sediment into clean, sterilised bottles to within $2\frac{1}{4}$ inches (57 mm) of the top of each bottle. Lightly stopper the bottles with sterilised, rinsed cork or plastic stoppers, or plug with cotton wool.

e) Pasteurise the cider vinegar by standing the bottles on a wooden board, thick cloth or folded newspaper placed in a large saucepan partly filled with water. Heat until hot – NOT boiling. Keep the temperature just off boiling for thirty minutes; then switch off heat and fasten sterilised, rinsed cork or plastic stoppers securely into bottles.

f) Label clearly and store for eight weeks to mature. Your cider vinegar is then ready to use.

Please remember to keep your cider vinegar well away from stocks of wine, beer and cider. The cider vinegar aroma can taint them and if any cider vinegar comes into contact with them, they too may convert to vinegar.

Clean and sterilise all equipment used.

24

CIDER SNAGS

You should encounter few snags in your cider making. Here are some snags to watch for – and the action to take to put things right.

Snag 1

The fermenting or maturing cider smells like vinegar and tastes bitter.

Action:

Your cider has been infected by the tiny vinegar fly (Drosophila Melanogaster). Your only action must be to convert fully the cider to excellent, health promoting cider vinegar, see page 98.

This snag should not occur when the fermenting or maturing cider is kept securely covered at all times.

Snag 2

The surface of the maturing cider is being slowly covered by a film of tiny white flecks of powder.

Action:

The cider has been infected by a species of wild yeast. Immediate action is necessary to prevent the alcohol being gradually turned into carbon dioxide and water.

a) Strain your cider through a sterilised, rinsed, finely-meshed sieve, piece of muslin or tights trimmed into a square with scissors. Discard the white flecks. To kill the bacteria, to each gallon (4½ litres) of infected cider; add the juice of one or two lemons OR 1 level teaspoon (5 mls) of sulphite solution (sodium metabisulphite mixed with water, see page 32) OR one crushed Campden tablet (sodium metabisulphite).

Snag 3

The cider has been matured for the period suggested in the recipe

and is ready for bottling or barrelling, but tastes insipid.
Action:

Add 1 level tablespoon of strained, brewed tea and the juice of one lemon OR one orange to each gallon (4½ litres) of cider before bottling or barrelling.

Snag 4

Your cider has been matured for the period suggested in the recipe and is ready for bottling or barrelling, but tastes too sharp and acidic.

Action:

Bottle or barrel the cider as it is. You may well find the acidity is balanced naturally by the time you wish to drink it, but if not add ½ level tablespoon of caster sugar OR 1 level tablespoon of pure honey to each 1 pint (½ litre) glass or tankard before serving. Pour the cider onto the caster sugar or pure honey and stir vigorously until dissolved. Then serve. The sweetness of the sugar or pure honey smooths and rounds the taste of your cider and removes its biting edge.

25

DRINK UP THEE ZIDER

Cider recipes in this book list ingredients required to make 1 gallon (4½ litres) of cider. Allowing for sediment discarded before bottling, this quantity will fill eight 1 pint (½ litre) home brew beer bottles.

Zider zeal

If you are a zealous cider maker, or intend to become one, and wish to make your cider in larger amounts than 1 gallon (4½ litres), you can buy brewing bins and narrow-necked glass and plastic vessels designed to hold up to 5½ gallons (25 litres) of fermenting or maturing home brew, see page 28.

Never be conservative

Do not get stuck in a rut with your cider making. Be adventurous and inventive – experiment!

You can add many single natural ingredients to enrich your cider's flavour and health enhancing properties. Pop an extra in while the cider ferments for 5 days in your bucket or brewing bin.

Among additives well worth trying separately are: fresh, rinsed rose petals – 4 oz (113 gms) or 1 oz (28 gms) dried; elderflower florets – 2 oz (56 gms) or ½ oz (14 gms) dried; dandelion heads – 4 oz (113 gms) or 1 oz (28 gms) dried; fresh, chopped peaches with stones discarded – 8 oz (227 gms); pure blackcurrant juice – 5 fl oz (142 mls); pure orange juice – 5 fl oz (142 mls); pure grapefruit juice – 5 fl oz (142 mls); pure passion fruit juice – 5 fl oz (142 mls) etc., etc.

All these items are available from your health food stockist.

Are you strong?

Be strong willed and resist the temptation to quaff your "real" cider too quickly. Remember its strength. Think of the morning after the night before!

GOOD HEALTH!

26

COOKING WITH CIDER

Bring your cooking to life with cider. Use your home-made cider to lend ordinary food extra health-giving goodness and appetizing appeal.

Think of the many ways you can employ cider to make your favourite meals even more exciting.

Here are a few ideas to get you started.

Cider ice cream

Make this delicious sweet by mixing your favourite ice cream with an equal amount of fresh whipped cream. Pour chilled cider over the mixed ice cream and whipped cream before serving.

Lentil soup – *serves 4*
Ingredients
Cider – ½ pint (284 mls)
Soft vegetable margarine – 1 oz (28 gms)
Carrot – 1
Onion – 1
Red lentils – ¼ pint (142 mls)
Sea salt and freshly ground black pepper – to your taste
Stock (stock cube) – ½ pint (284 mls)
Method

Melt margarine in saucepan. Add lentils and thinly sliced vegetables. Cook over low heat until margarine has been absorbed. Add cider and stock; salt and pepper. Simmer until vegetables and lentils are cooked. Then rub the soup through a finely meshed sieve and serve.

Liver and onion pudding – *serves 2–3*
Ingredients
Cider – 1 pint (½ litre)

Soft vegetable margarine – ¼ lb (113 gms)
Oats – 1 lb (454 gms)
Onion – 1
Pig's liver – ½ lb (227 gms)
Sea salt and freshly ground black pepper to your taste
Method

Put oats in mixing bowl and cover with cider. While the cider is being absorbed by the oats, mince liver and onion; season with salt and pepper to your taste and then mix well with oats and margarine. Turn mixture into greased basin. Cover top with cooking foil and place in a steamer. Steam for 2 hours. Serve with potatoes and peas.

*TIP

Mixed fruit dessert

Serve your favourite fresh fruit topped with a liberal measure of chilled cider. Add ice cream as an appetizing bonus.

*TIP

Poached fruit with cider

Keep cooked fruit whole by poaching in cider. Prepare fruit of your choice and place in an oven proof dish. Add some cider and cover. Poach in moderate oven, gas no. 4 (350°F). When cooked, serve sweetened with pure honey.

*TIP

Sausages and bacon

For fuller flavour poach sausages and lean bacon in cider instead of frying.

Tripe supper dish – *serves 2-3*
Ingredients
Cider – ½ pint (284 mls)
Dry crumbs from wholemeal bread – 1 cup (finely grated)
Free range egg – 1
Clove of garlic – 1
Green pepper – 1
Pure vegetable oil – sufficient for frying
Onions – 2
Tomatoes – 1 lb (½ kg)
Tripe – 1½ lbs (680 gms)
Sea salt and freshly ground black pepper – to your taste

Method

Simmer tripe for about 45 minutes in cider. Fry finely chopped onions, garlic and green pepper until onions are lightly browned. Then add sliced tomatoes and salt and pepper to your taste. Simmer for 10 minutes. Cut tripe into 2 inch (51 mm) squares; dip tripe squares in beaten egg, and roll in breadcrumbs. Fry in vegetable oil until golden brown. Serve with the onions, green pepper and tomatoes.

27

CIDER CUPS

Summer cups

Cider cups offer you and your friends a long, refreshing and revitalizing drink on sizzling hot summer's days.

A small measure of vodka can be added to any of these recipes if you desire a strong summer party punch.

Adjust the quantity of ingredients in these recipes to suit the amount you or your guests wish to drink.

Egg flip cider cup

Traditional, nourishing and satisfying cider cup. Also an ancient and popular remedy for unexpected summer colds or influenza.

Ingredients: To make 1 pint (½ litre)

Chilled cider – 1 pint (½ litre)

Free range eggs – 2

Pure honey – 2 level tablespoons

Method

Mix all ingredients briskly until the cider is frothy. Then serve in a chilled tankard or glass.

Fruit cider cup

Delightful, thirst quenching light drink.

*Use only pure orange juice bought from your health food stockist.

Ingredients: To make 2 pints (1¼ litres)

Chilled cider – 1 pint (½ litre)

Chilled mineral water – ½ pint (284 mls)

  or chilled soda water – ½ pint (284 mls)

Chilled pure orange juice – ½ pint (284 mls)

Raspberries – ½ lb (227 gms)

  or strawberries – ½ lb (227 gms)

Lemon – 6 thin slices
Cucumber – 6 thin slices
Ice – 6 cubes
Method

Wash fruit in cold water. Remove and discard stalks and any diseased parts. Place in a bowl and crush. Add all other ingredients and mix well. Cover and leave for 20 minutes; then serve in chilled tankards or glasses. Include some fruit in each serving.

Pineapple cider cup

Cooling, invigorating beverage. Ideal for a sultry summer's day.

*Use only pure pineapple juice bought from your health food stockist.

Ingredients: To make 2 pints (1¼ litres)
Chilled cider – 1 pint (½ litre)
Chilled mineral water – ½ pint (284 mls)
   or chilled soda water – ½ pint (284 mls)
Chilled pure pineapple juice – ½ pint (284 mls)
Pure honey – 2 level tablespoons
Method

Mix all ingredients together in a bowl and serve with ice cubes in chilled tankards or glasses.

Raspberry cider cup

Beautiful, decadent and welcome summer cider cup.

Ingredients: To make 2 pints (1¼ litres)
Chilled cider – 1 pint (½ litre)
Chilled white wine – 1 pint (½ litre)
   or chilled rosé wine – 1 pint (½ litre)
Raspberries – ½ lb (227 gms)
Pure honey – 2 heaped tablespoons
Ice cream – 1 heaped tablespoon per glass
Ice cubes – 6
Method

Wash raspberries in cold water. Remove and discard stalks and any diseased parts. Place in a bowl and crush. Add all other ingredients EXCEPT ice cream. Cover bowl and leave for 20 minutes; then serve in chilled large glasses. Include some raspberries in each serving and float a heaped tablespoon of ice cream on the surface of each drink.

28

QUICK INDEX TO CIDER MAKING PRINCIPLES AND METHODS

29

CIDER RECIPES

COUNTRY CIDER
Olde English Cider

Rich, wholesome cider. Unique, delicious flavour. Full of vitamins and goodness.

Ready to drink 8 weeks after being bottled or barrelled (about 5 months after it has finished fermenting).

Alcohol content about 7% alcohol by volume (12% proof).

*Use pure apple juice bought from your health food stockist.

Ingredients: To make 1 gallon (4½ litres)
Pure apple juice – 3½ pints (2 litres)
Mixed sweet and bitter apples – 3¼ lbs (1½ kgs)
Pears – 2¼ lbs (1 kg)
Root ginger – 1 oz (28 gms)
Pure honey – 9 oz (255 gms)
　　or granulated sugar – 8 oz (227 gms)
Brewed tea, strong – 1 level tablespoon
Pure lemon juice – 1 level tablespoon
Pure orange juice – 2 level tablespoons
All-purpose wine yeast starter bottle (see page 93)
　　or all-purpose dried wine yeast
　　or all-purpose liquid natural wine yeast
and
Water to 1 gallon (4½ litres)
Method
a) Pour the pure apple juice bought from your health food stockist into a sterilised, rinsed plastic (food grade) bucket or brewing bin. Cover.

b) Wash apples and pears in warm water. Cut out and discard diseased parts. Chop the apples and pears into chunks. Do not remove skins, cores or pips as these contain much goodness and contribute considerably to this cider's full flavour.

c) Mince apple and pear chunks with your kitchen mincer. Let the juice and minced apple and pear pulp run into your bucket or bin. Cover.

d) Bruise root ginger by crushing with a rolling pin or hammer.

e) Simmer about 2 pints (1¼ litres) of water in a saucepan and add bruised ginger. Cover and simmer gently for 15 minutes. Then add the pure honey OR granulated sugar and stir until dissolved. Cover and allow to cool. When cool, remove and discard root ginger and add liquid to apple and pear juice and pulp in bucket or bin. Cover.

f) Make tea, strain and allow to cool, or use strained cold tea from an earlier brew. Discard leaves or bag. Then add to bucket or bin. Cover.

g) Extract juice from lemon and orange and pour into bucket or bin.

h) Add the activated wine yeast from your starter bottle, or the quantity recommended by the manufacturer of the dried wine yeast, or liquid natural wine yeast.

i) Top up with cold water to the total quantity of cider you require.

j) Check you have allowed at least 2 inches (51 mm)–4 inches (102 mm) at the top of your bucket or bin for frothing and foaming.

k) Cover and keep somewhere warm for 5 days, about 18°C (64°F) is ideal.

l) Stir juice and pulp twice daily.

After 5 days

a) Strain into a sterilised, rinsed 1 gallon (4½ litre) narrow-necked glass or plastic vessel. If necessary, top up to the neck with cold water.

b) Fit a sterilised, rinsed bored cork or rubber bung and an air lock filled with water, or preferably sulphite solution (sodium metabisulphite mixed with water, see page 32) OR plug the neck with cotton wool OR cover the mouth with a 7 inch (178 mm) square of sterilised, rinsed polythene; smoothed tightly over the top of the vessel and secured around the neck with an elastic band, string or strong thread.

Keep the cider in a warm place until it has finished fermenting.

This can take from 12–17 days.

Judging when fermentation has finished

a) Air locks

If you have fitted an air lock, bubbles of carbon dioxide gas pass up through the water or sulphite solution in the air lock while your cider is fermenting. As fermentation slows the bubbles become less frequent and eventually stop altogether. This is an indication that fermentation has ceased.

b) Cotton wool or covering square of polythene

Watch the surface of your cider. When bubbling has ceased and your cider is beginning to fall clear from the top downwards, your cider has probably finished fermenting.

Checks

Pour or syphon a little cider into a glass and take a sip to see if your cider tastes dry (non-sweet). If there is no hint of sweetness; no bubbles of carbon dioxide gas and the cider is not fizzy on your tongue, it has finished fermenting.

When you are satisfied your cider has finished fermenting:

a) Sterilise and rinse your plastic (food grade) bucket or brewing bin and syphon the cider from the 1 gallon (4½ litre) narrow-necked vessel into your bucket or bin. Cover.

b) Rinse the sediment from your 1 gallon (4½ litre) vessel. Sterilise and rinse the vessel and then pour the cider from your bucket or bin back into the 1 gallon (4½ litre) vessel through a sterilised, rinsed polythene funnel.

c) Top up to the neck with cold water or cider from a previously made batch.

d) Plug the neck with a sterilised, rinsed cork or rubber bung. Occasionally, a small fermentation of residual natural sugar (fructose and glucose) or granulated sugar (sucrose) in the cider takes place and forces up the cork or rubber bung. To guard against this possibility, cover the bung with a 7 inch (178 mm) square of sterilised, rinsed polythene; smoothed tightly over the bung and secured around the vessel's neck with two elastic bands (two in case one perishes and snaps). If a small fermentation does occur, the bung rises to release the carbon dioxide gas but does not fly off, exposing your cider to possible bacterial infection. Check bungs periodically and re-fasten where necessary. Store somewhere cool to clear and mature, about 10°C (50°F) to 13°C (55°F) is ideal.

Your olde English cider should be clear and ready for bottling or barrelling (see page 95) about 3 months after it has finished fermenting and been stored to clear and mature.

After being bottled or barrelled, your olde English still or sparkling cider should be allowed a further 8 weeks to develop and condition before being served.

Olde English still cider remains in excellent condition in bottles for up to 6 months. It is not suitable for barrelling.

Olde English sparkling cider remains in excellent condition in bottles for up to 10 months. When stored in a plastic pressure barrel it should stay in good condition for about 7 months, although its quality may begin a slow decline once the first few pints have been drawn off.

Rogue's Cider

If you want to make good quality cider without fuss and bother and with only a minimum of effort then you are a rogue, and this is the very cider for you.

Ready to drink 8 weeks after being bottled or barrelled (about 5 months after it has finished fermenting).

Alcohol content about 7% alcohol by volume (12% proof).

*Use pure apple juice bought from your health food stockist.

Ingredients: To make 1 gallon (4½ litres)

Pure apple juice – 3½ pints (2 litres)

Mixed sweet and bitter apples – 2¼ lbs (1 kg)

Pure honey – 11 oz (312 gms)

  or granulated sugar – 10 oz (283 gms)

Brewed tea, strong – 1 level tablespoon

Pure lemon juice – 1 level tablespoon

All-purpose wine yeast starter bottle (see page 93)

  or all-purpose dried wine yeast

  or all-purpose liquid natural wine yeast

and

Water to 1 gallon (4½ litres)

Method

a) Pour the pure apple juice bought from your health food stockist into a sterilised, rinsed plastic (food grade) bucket or brewing bin. Cover.

b) Wash apples in warm water. Cut out and discard diseased parts. Chop the apples into chunks. Do not remove skins, cores or pips as these contain much goodness and contribute considerably to this cider's full flavour.

c) Mince apple chunks with your kitchen mincer. Let the juice and minced apple pulp run into your bucket or bin. Cover.

d) Simmer 1 pint (½ litre) of water in a saucepan and dissolve the pure honey OR granulated sugar. Cover and allow to cool. When cool, add to apple juice and pulp in bucket or bin. Cover.

e) Make tea, strain and allow to cool, or use strained cold tea from an earlier brew. Discard leaves or bag. Then add to bucket or bin. Cover.

f) Extract juice from lemon and pour into bucket or bin.

g) Add the activated wine yeast from your starter bottle, or the quantity recommended by the manufacturer of the dried wine yeast, or liquid natural wine yeast.

h) Top up with cold water to the total quantity of cider you require.

i) Check you have allowed at least 2 inches (51 mm)–4 inches (102 mm) at the top of your bucket or bin for frothing and foaming.

j) Cover and keep somewhere warm for 5 days, about 18°C (64°F) is ideal.

k) Stir juice and pulp twice daily.

After 5 days

a) Strain into a sterilised, rinsed 1 gallon (4½ litre) narrow-necked glass or plastic vessel. If necessary, top up to the neck with cold water.

b) Fit a sterilised, rinsed bored cork or rubber bung and an air lock filled with water, or preferably sulphite solution (sodium metabisulphite mixed with water, see page 32) OR plug the neck with cotton wool OR cover the mouth with a 7 inch (178 mm) square of sterilised, rinsed polythene; smoothed tightly over the top of the vessel and secured around the neck with an elastic band, string or strong thread.

Keep the cider in a warm place until it has finished fermenting. This can take from 12–17 days.

Judging when fermentation has finished

a) Air locks

If you have fitted an air lock, bubbles of carbon dioxide gas pass up through the water or sulphite solution in the air lock while your cider is fermenting. As fermentation slows the bubbles become less frequent and eventually stop altogether. This is an indication that fermentation has ceased.

b) Cotton wool or covering square of polythene

Watch the surface of your cider. When bubbling has ceased and your cider is beginning to fall clear from the top downwards, your cider has probably finished fermenting.

Checks

Pour or syphon a little cider into a glass and take a sip to see if your cider tastes dry (non-sweet). If there is no hint of sweetness; no bubbles of carbon dioxide gas and the cider is not fizzy on your tongue, it has finished fermenting.

When you are satisfied your cider has finished fermenting:

a) Sterilise and rinse your plastic (food grade) bucket or brewing bin and syphon the cider from the 1 gallon (4½ litre) narrow-necked vessel into your bucket or bin. Cover.

b) Rinse the sediment from your 1 gallon (4½ litre) vessel. Sterilise and rinse the vessel and then pour the cider from your bucket or bin back into the 1 gallon (4½ litre) vessel through a sterilised, rinsed polythene funnel.

c) Top up to the neck with cold water or cider from a previously made batch.

d) Plug the neck with a sterilised, rinsed cork or rubber bung. Occasionally, a small fermentation of residual natural sugar (fructose and glucose) or granulated sugar (sucrose) in the cider takes place and forces up the cork or rubber bung. To guard against this possibility, cover the bung with a 7 inch (178 mm) square of sterilised, rinsed polythene; smoothed tightly over the bung and secured around the vessel's neck with two elastic bands (two in case one perishes and snaps). If a small fermentation does occur, the bung rises to release the carbon dioxide gas but does not fly off, exposing your cider to possible bacterial infection. Check bungs periodically and re-fasten where necessary. Store somewhere cool to clear and mature, about 10°C (50°F) to 13°C (55°F) is ideal.

Your rogue's cider should be clear and ready for bottling or barrelling (see page 95) about 3 months after it has finished fermenting and been stored to clear and mature.

After being bottled or barrelled, your rogue's still or sparkling cider should be allowed a further 8 weeks to develop and condition before being served.

Rogue's still cider remains in excellent condition in bottles for up to 6 months. It is not suitable for barrelling.

Rogue's sparkling cider remains in excellent condition in bottles for up to 10 months. When stored in a plastic pressure barrel it should stay in good condition for about 7 months, although its quality may begin a slow decline once the first few pints have been drawn off.

Celtic Cider

Real cider, made exclusively from pure apple juice. Full of rich apple goodness. Ready to drink 8 weeks after being bottled or barrelled (about 6 months after it has finished fermenting).

Alcohol content about 7% alcohol by volume (12% proof).

Please Note

For this recipe you need access to a fruit press. If you have a large supply of apples and wish to make cider for regular consumption, you may like to buy your own press. Small fruit presses are sold by your local homebrew stockist. As a sturdy press should last your lifetime, the cost is reasonable.

To make 1 gallon (4½ litres) of 100% natural cider from pure juice pressed from apples, you require about 20 lbs (9 kgs) of mixed sweet and bitter apples. The best combination is about 10 lbs (4½ kgs) of assorted sweet apples and about 10 lbs (4½ kgs) of assorted bitter apples, but you can successfully use any selection of sweet and bitter windfalls.

Ingredients: To make 1 gallon (4½ litres)

Natural, sugar-free recipe

Mixed sweet and bitter apples – about 20 lbs (9 kgs)

Brewed tea, strong – 1 level tablespoon

Pure lemon juice – 1 level tablespoon

All-purpose wine yeast starter bottle (see page 93)

    or all-purpose dried wine yeast

    or all-purpose liquid natural wine yeast

Method

a) Wash apples in warm water. Cut out and discard diseased parts. Chop the apples into chunks. There is no need to remove skins, cores or pips.

b) Extract juice from apples with your fruit press. Let the juice run into a sterilised, rinsed plastic (food grade) bucket or brewing bin. Cover. Discard apple pulp.

c) Make tea, strain and allow to cool, or use strained cold tea from an earlier brew. Discard leaves or bag. Then add to apple juice in bucket or bin. Cover.

d) Extract juice from lemon and pour into bucket or bin.

e) Add the activated wine yeast from your starter bottle, or the quantity recommended by the manufacturer of the dried wine yeast, or liquid natural wine yeast.

f) Top up with pure pressed apple juice to the total quantity of cider you require.

g) Check you have allowed at least 2 inches (51 mm)–4 inches (102 mm) at the top of your bucket or bin for frothing and foaming.

h) Cover and keep somewhere warm for 5 days, about 18°C (64°F) is ideal.

i) Stir juice twice daily.

After 5 days

a) Strain into a sterilised, rinsed 1 gallon (4½ litre) narrow-necked glass or plastic vessel. If necessary, top up to the neck with pure apple juice pressed from apples or bought from your health food stockist.

b) Fit a sterilised, rinsed bored cork or rubber bung and an air lock filled with water, or preferably sulphite solution (sodium metabisulphite mixed with water, see page 32) OR plug the neck with cotton wool OR cover the mouth with a 7 inch (178 mm) square of sterilised, rinsed polythene; smoothed tightly over the top of the vessel and secured around the neck with an elastic band, string or strong thread.

Keep the cider in a warm place until it has finished fermenting. This can take from 12–17 days.

Judging when fermentation has finished

a) Air locks

If you have fitted an air lock, bubbles of carbon dioxide gas pass up through the water or sulphite solution in the air lock while your cider is fermenting. As fermentation slows the bubbles become less frequent and eventually stop altogether. This is an indication that fermentation has ceased.

b) Cotton wool or covering square of polythene

Watch the surface of your cider. When bubbling has ceased and your cider is beginning to fall clear from the top downwards, your cider has probably finished fermenting.

Checks

Pour or syphon a little cider into a glass and take a sip to see if your cider tastes dry (non-sweet). If there is no hint of sweetness; no bubbles of carbon dioxide gas and the cider is not fizzy on your tongue, it has finished fermenting.

When you are satisfied your cider has finished fermenting:

a) Sterilise and rinse your plastic (food grade) bucket or brewing bin and syphon the cider from the 1 gallon (4½ litre) narrow-necked vessel into your bucket or bin. Cover.

b) Rinse the sediment from your 1 gallon (4½ litre) vessel. Sterilise and rinse the vessel and then pour the cider from your bucket or bin back into the 1 gallon (4½ litre) vessel through a sterilised, rinsed polythene funnel.

c) Top up to the neck with cold water or cider from a previously made batch.

d) Plug the neck with a sterilised, rinsed cork or rubber bung. Occasionally, a small fermentation of residual natural sugar (fructose and glucose) or granulated sugar (sucrose) in the cider takes place and forces up the cork or rubber bung. To guard against this possibility, cover the bung with a 7 inch (178 mm) square of sterilised, rinsed polythene; smoothed tightly over the bung and secured around the vessel's neck with two elastic bands (two in case one perishes and snaps). If a small fermentation does occur, the bung rises to release the carbon dioxide gas but does not fly off, exposing your cider to possible bacterial infection. Check bungs periodically and re-fasten where necessary. Store somewhere cool to clear and mature, about 10°C (50°F) to 13°C (55°F) is ideal.

Your Celtic cider should be clear and ready for bottling or barrelling (see page 95) about 4 months after it has finished fermenting and been stored to clear and mature.

After being bottled or barrelled, your Celtic still or sparkling cider should be allowed a further 8 weeks to develop and condition before being served.

Celtic still cider remains in excellent condition in bottles for up to

6 months. It is not suitable for barrelling.

Celtic sparkling cider remains in excellent condition in bottles for up to 10 months. When stored in a plastic pressure barrel it should stay in good condition for about 7 months, although its quality may begin a slow decline once the first few pints have been drawn off.

Golden Cider

Golden, glowing drink. Easily made cider, rewarding in its excellence. Ready to drink 8 weeks after being bottled or barrelled (about 5 months after it has finished fermenting).

Alcohol content about 7% alcohol by volume (12% proof).

*Use pure apple juice bought from your health food stockist.

Ingredients: To make 1 gallon (4½ litres)

Pure apple juice – 3½ pints (2 litres)

Mixed sweet and bitter apples – 5 lbs (2¼ kgs)

Pure honey – 9 oz (255 gms)

　or granulated sugar – 8 oz (227 gms)

Brewed tea, strong – 1 level tablespoon

Pure lemon juice – 1 level tablespoon

All-purpose wine yeast starter bottle (see page 93)

　or all-purpose dried wine yeast

　or all-purpose liquid natural wine yeast

and

Water to 1 gallon (4½ litres)

Method

a) Pour the pure apple juice bought from your health food stockist into a sterilised, rinsed plastic (food grade) bucket or brewing bin. Cover.

b) Wash apples in warm water. Cut out and discard diseased parts. Chop the apples into chunks. Do not remove skins, cores or pips as these contain much goodness and contribute considerably to this cider's full flavour.

c) Mince apple chunks with your kitchen mincer. Let the juice and minced apple pulp run into your bucket or bin. Cover.

d) Simmer 1 pint (½ litre) of water in a saucepan and dissolve the pure honey OR granulated sugar. Cover and allow to cool. When cool, add to apple juice and pulp in bucket or bin. Cover.

e) Make tea, strain and allow to cool, or use strained cold tea from an earlier brew. Discard leaves or bag. Then add to bucket or bin. Cover.

f) Extract juice from lemon and pour into bucket or bin.

g) Add the activated wine yeast from your starter bottle, or the quantity recommended by the manufacturer of the dried wine yeast, or liquid natural wine yeast.

h) Top up with cold water to the total quantity of cider you require.

i) Check you have allowed at least 2 inches (51 mm)–4 inches (102 mm) at the top of your bucket or bin for frothing and foaming.

j) Cover and keep somewhere warm for 5 days, about 18°C (64°F) is ideal.

k) Stir juice and pulp twice daily.

After 5 days

a) Strain into a sterilised, rinsed 1 gallon (4½ litre) narrow-necked glass or plastic vessel. If necessary, top up to the neck with cold water.

b) Fit a sterilised, rinsed bored cork or rubber bung and an air lock filled with water, or preferably sulphite solution (sodium metabisulphite mixed with water, see page 32) OR plug the neck with cotton wool OR cover the mouth with a 7 inch (178 mm) square of sterilised, rinsed polythene; smoothed tightly over the top of the vessel and secured around the neck with an elastic band, string or strong thread.

Keep the cider in a warm place until it has finished fermenting. This can take from 12–17 days.

Judging when fermentation has finished

a) Air locks

If you have fitted an air lock, bubbles of carbon dioxide gas pass up through the water or sulphite solution in the air lock while your cider is fermenting. As fermentation slows the bubbles become less frequent and eventually stop altogether. This is an indication that fermentation has ceased.

b) Cotton wool or covering square of polythene

Watch the surface of your cider. When bubbling has ceased and your cider is beginning to fall clear from the top downwards, your cider has probably finished fermenting.

Checks

Pour or syphon a little cider into a glass and take a sip to see if your cider tastes dry (non-sweet). If there is no hint of sweetness; no bubbles of carbon dioxide gas and the cider is not fizzy on your tongue, it has finished fermenting.

When you are satisfied your cider has finished fermenting:

a) Sterilise and rinse your plastic (food grade) bucket or brewing bin and syphon the cider from the 1 gallon (4½ litre) narrow-necked vessel into your bucket or bin. Cover.

b) Rinse the sediment from your 1 gallon (4½ litre) vessel. Sterilise and rinse the vessel and then pour the cider from your bucket or bin back into the 1 gallon (4½ litre) vessel through a sterilised, rinsed polythene funnel.

c) Top up to the neck with cold water or cider from a previously made batch.

d) Plug the neck with a sterilised, rinsed cork or rubber bung. Occasionally, a small fermentation of residual natural sugar (fructose and glucose) or granulated sugar (sucrose) in the cider takes place and forces up the cork or rubber bung. To guard against this possibility, cover the bung with a 7 inch (178 mm) square of sterilised, rinsed polythene; smoothed tightly over the bung and secured around the vessel's neck with two elastic bands (two in case one perishes and snaps). If a small fermentation does occur, the bung rises to release the carbon dioxide gas but does not fly off, exposing your cider to possible bacterial infection. Check bungs periodically and re-fasten where necessary. Store somewhere cool to clear and mature, about 10°C (50°F) to 13°C (55°F) is ideal.

Your golden cider should be clear and ready for bottling or barrelling (see page 95) about 3 months after it has finished fermenting and been stored to clear and mature.

After being bottled or barrelled, your golden still or sparkling cider should be allowed a further 8 weeks to develop and condition before being served.

Golden still cider remains in excellent condition in bottles for up to 6 months. It is not suitable for barrelling.

Golden sparkling cider remains in excellent condition in bottles for up to 10 months. When stored in a plastic pressure barrel it should stay in good condition for about 7 months, although its quality may begin a slow decline once the first few pints have been drawn off.

Scrumpy

For lovers of strong, rough cider. Meant to be drunk while young and cloudy, though it will clear and mellow if left to mature for 3 months after it has finished fermenting, before being bottled or barrelled.

Ready to drink as scrumpy 5 weeks after being bottled or barrelled (about 10 weeks after it has finished fermenting).

HANGOVER WARNING

Sip scrumpy by the wine glass full. It has a true scrumpy's west country kick. You have been warned!

Alcohol content about 8% alcohol by volume (14% proof).

*Use pure apple juice bought from your health food stockist.

Ingredients: To make 1 gallon (4½ litres)

Pure apple juice – 3½ pints (2 litres)

Mixed sweet and bitter apples – 3¼ lbs (1½ kgs)

Pure honey – 1 lb (454 gms)

   or granulated sugar – 14 oz (397 gms)

Brewed tea, strong – 1 level tablespoon

Pure lemon juice – 1 level tablespoon

All-purpose wine yeast starter bottle (see page 93)

   or all-purpose dried wine yeast

   or all-purpose liquid natural wine yeast

and

Water to 1 gallon (4½ litres)

Method

a) Pour the pure apple juice bought from your health food stockist into a sterilised, rinsed plastic (food grade) bucket or brewing bin. Cover.

b) Wash apples in warm water. Cut out and discard diseased parts. Chop the apples into chunks. Do not remove skins, cores or pips as these contain much goodness and contribute considerably to this scrumpy's full flavour.

c) Mince apple chunks with your kitchen mincer. Let the juice and minced apple pulp run into your bucket or bin. Cover.

d) Simmer 1 pint (½ litre) of water in a saucepan and dissolve the pure honey OR granulated sugar. Cover and allow to cool. When cool, add to apple juice and pulp in bucket or bin. Cover.

e) Make tea, strain and allow to cool, or use strained cold tea from an earlier brew. Discard leaves or bag. Then add to bucket or bin. Cover.

f) Extract juice from lemon and pour into bucket or bin.

g) Add the activated wine yeast from your starter bottle, or the quantity recommended by the manufacturer of the dried wine yeast, or liquid natural wine yeast.

h) Top up with cold water to the total quantity of scrumpy you require.

i) Check you have allowed at least 2 inches (51 mm)–4 inches (102 mm) at the top of your bucket or bin for frothing and foaming.

j) Cover and keep somewhere warm for 5 days, about 18°C (64°F) is ideal.

k) Stir juice and pulp twice daily.

After 5 days

a) Strain into a sterilised, rinsed 1 gallon (4½ litre) narrow-necked glass or plastic vessel. If necessary, top up to the neck with cold water.

b) Fit a sterilised, rinsed bored cork or rubber bung and an air lock filled with water, or preferably sulphite solution (sodium metabisulphite mixed with water, see page 32) OR plug the neck with cotton wool OR cover the mouth with a 7 inch (178 mm) square of sterilised, rinsed polythene; smoothed tightly over the top of the vessel and secured around the neck with an elastic band, string or strong thread.

Keep the scrumpy in a warm place until it has finished fermenting. This can take from 14–19 days.

Judging when fermentation has finished

a) Air locks

If you have fitted an air lock, bubbles of carbon dioxide gas pass up through the water or sulphite solution in the air lock while your scrumpy is fermenting. As fermentation slows the bubbles become less frequent and eventually stop altogether. This is an indication that fermentation has ceased.

b) Cotton wool or covering square of polythene

Watch the surface of your scrumpy. When bubbling has ceased

and your scrumpy is beginning to fall clear from the top downwards, your scrumpy has probably finished fermenting.

Checks

Pour or syphon a little scrumpy into a glass and take a sip to see if your scrumpy tastes dry (non-sweet). If there is no hint of sweetness; no bubbles of carbon dioxide gas and the scrumpy is not fizzy on your tongue, it has finished fermenting.

When you are satisfied your scrumpy has finished fermenting:

a) Sterilise and rinse your plastic (food grade) bucket or brewing bin and syphon the scrumpy from the 1 gallon (4½ litre) narrow-necked vessel into your bucket or bin. Cover.

b) Rinse the sediment from your 1 gallon (4½ litre) vessel. Sterilise and rinse the vessel and then pour the scrumpy from your bucket or bin back into the 1 gallon (4½ litre) vessel through a sterilised, rinsed polythene funnel.

c) Top up to the neck with cold water or scrumpy from a previously made batch.

d) Plug the neck with a sterilised, rinsed cork or rubber bung. Occasionally, a small fermentation of residual natural sugar (fructose and glucose) or granulated sugar (sucrose) in the scrumpy takes place and forces up the cork or rubber bung. To guard against this possibility, cover the bung with a 7 inch (178 mm) square of sterilised, rinsed polythene; smoothed tightly over the bung and secured around the vessel's neck with two elastic bands (two in case one perishes and snaps). If a small fermentation does occur, the bung rises to release the carbon dioxide gas but does not fly off, exposing your scrumpy to possible bacterial infection. Check bungs periodically and re-fasten where necessary. Store somewhere cool to clear and mature, about 10°C (50°F) to 13°C (55°F) is ideal.

Your scrumpy is ready for bottling or barrelling (see page 95) 5 weeks after it has finished fermenting and been stored to clear and mature.

After being bottled or barrelled, your still or sparkling scrumpy should be allowed a further 5 weeks to develop and condition before being served.

Still scrumpy ought really be drunk young but remains in excellent condition in bottles for up to 7 months. It is not suitable for barrelling.

Sparkling scrumpy ought really be drunk young but remains in excellent condition in bottles for up to 12 months. When stored in a plastic pressure barrel it should stay in good condition for about 8 months, although its quality may begin a slow decline once the first few pints have been drawn off.

Also by Ian Ball

Wine Making
The Natural Way

Step-by-step natural methods can produce a splendid array of country-style wines for an outlay of only pence per bottle. A wine to complement every repast can be spread evenly throughout the year using his planner; a drinkable wine on your table in a few weeks.

These simple recipes minimise the need for special equipment. Wholesale fruits, flowers, vegetables, etc., are free for gathering or can be bought in season while prices are low. Using them as close to their original form as possible safeguards healing properties and retains valuable oils and scents while maximum flavour, vitamins and goodness are extracted. Making the craft easy to learn and fun, Ian Ball ensures your year-round supply of refreshing wines.

*   *   *   *Many wine makers desire sugar-free recipes*   *   *   *
*for enhanced health and enjoyment. Pure honey
and grape juice feature as a natural alternative
in all these recipes.*

Also by Ian Ball

Wine Making
With Herbs

Reveals how you can impart exciting and delicious *new* flavours to economical home-made wines and liqueurs using fresh and/ or dried herbs, which you may gather yourself or obtain from herbalists, garden centres, health-food and home-brew stockists. Learn about herbs and their traditional medicinal qualities, beneficial effects and popular uses.

Easy-to-follow instructions are detailed and comprehensive. Brim-full of brilliant new ideas, hints, tips, advice on equipment, optional use of chemicals and notes on each wine's final bouquet, colour, flavour and alcoholic strength.

Again – *natural*, health-giving alternatives are given so you don't need to add sugar or chemicals. Substitute pure fruit juice, and/or grape juice and honey instead of sugar.

Easymade Wine & Country Drinks

Mrs Gennery-Taylor's famous country recipes will bring lovely wines to your table without the need for expensive equipment. A clever **wine calendar** tells you when to make each wine throughout the year and a **standard basic recipe** is included in case you want to try your luck with some unusual wine for which there is no detailed recipe. Also contains lots of ideas for delicious non-alcoholic country drinks.

Home Winemaking The Right Way

Kenneth Hawkins has been producing home-made wines, beers and liqueurs for over 20 years and has taught at evening classes. Here are 55 of his favourite recipes, many of which have won awards. Includes analysis of how and why various types of wine differ and shows how to train your palate to judge their relative qualities – the key to mastery both of what to do when in trouble and of the subtle adjustments which can transform a moderate wine into an award-winner.

RIGHT WAY
PUBLISHING POLICY

HOW WE SELECT TITLES

RIGHT WAY consider carefully every deserving manuscript. Where an author is an authority on his subject but an inexperienced writer, we provide first-class editorial help. The standards we set make sure that every **RIGHT WAY** book is practical, easy to understand, concise, informative and delightful to read. Our specialist artists are skilled at creating simple illustrations which augment the text wherever necessary.

CONSISTENT QUALITY

At every reprint our books are updated where appropriate, giving our authors the opportunity to include new information.

FAST DELIVERY

We sell **RIGHT WAY** books to the best bookshops throughout the world. It may be that your bookseller has run out of stock of a particular title. If so, he can order more from us at any time – we have a fine reputation for "same day" despatch, and we supply any order, however small (even a single copy), to any bookseller who has an account with us. We prefer you to buy from your bookseller, as this reminds him of the strong underlying public demand for **RIGHT WAY** books. Readers who live in remote places, or who are housebound, or whose local bookseller is unco-operative, can order direct from us by post.

FREE

If you would like an up-to-date list of all **RIGHT WAY** titles currently available, please send a stamped self-addressed envelope to

ELLIOT RIGHT WAY BOOKS,
KINGSWOOD, SURREY, KT20 6TD, U.K.